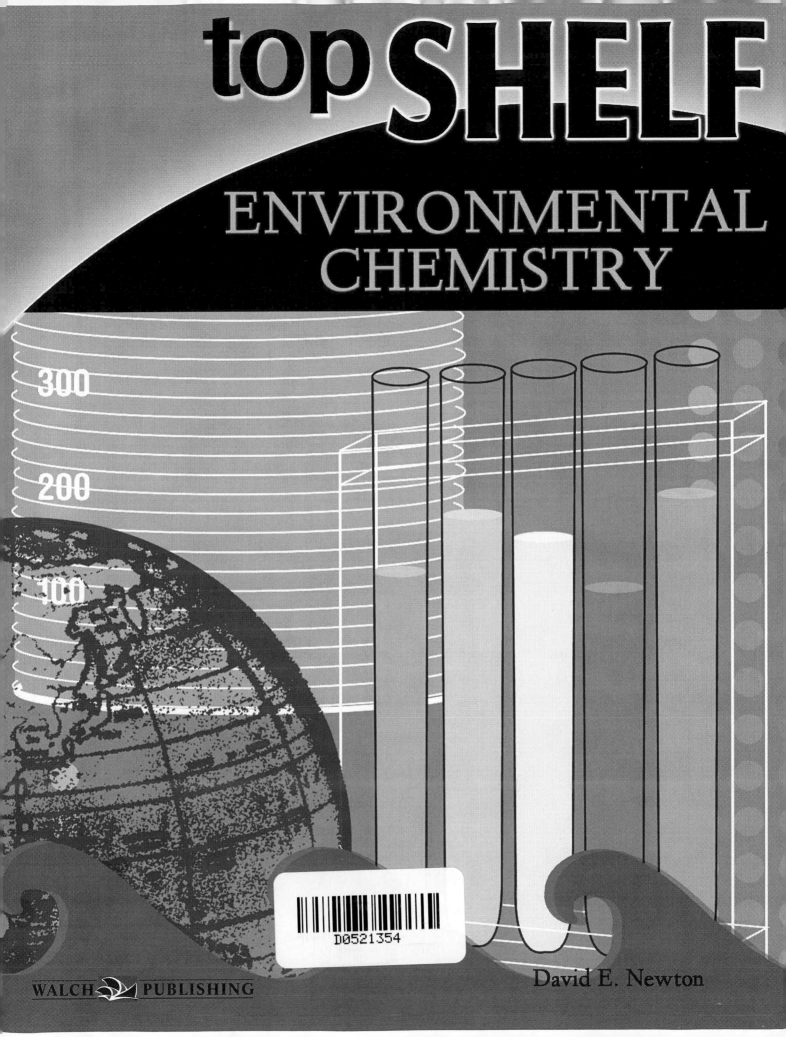

top SHELF
ENVIRONMENTAL CHEMISTRY

300

200

100

David E. Newton

WALCH PUBLISHING

1   2   3   4   5   6   7   8   9   10

ISBN 0-8251-5045-0

Copyright © 1991, 2004

Walch Publishing

P.O. Box 658 • Portland, Maine 04104-0658

walch.com

Printed in the United States of America

Contents

National Science Standards for High School

The goals for school science that underlie the National Science Education Standards are to educate students who are able to

- experience the richness and excitement of knowing about and understanding the natural world;

- use appropriate scientific processes and principles in making personal decisions;

- engage intelligently in public discourse and debate about matters of scientific and technological concern; and

- increase their economic productivity in their careers through using knowledge, understanding, and skills they have acquired as scientifically literate individuals.

These goals define a scientifically literate society. The standards for content define what the scientifically literate person should know, understand, and be able to do after 13 years of school science.

The four years of high-school science are typically devoted to earth and space science in ninth grade, biology in tenth grade, chemistry in eleventh grade, and physics in twelfth grade. Students between grades 9 and 12 are expected to learn about modeling, evidence, organization, and measurement, and to achieve an understanding of the history of science. They should also accumulate information about scientific inquiry, especially through laboratory activity.

Our series, *Top Shelf Science,* addresses not only the national standards, but also the underlying concepts that must be understood before the national standards issues can be fully explored. National standards are addressed in specific tests for college-bound students, such as the SAT II, the ACT, and the CLEP. We hope that you will find the readings and activities useful as general information as well as in preparation for higher-level coursework and testing. For additional books in the *Top Shelf Science* series, visit our web site at walch.com.

To the Teacher

Strictly speaking, environmental chemistry is the chemistry of the physical and biological environment, as well as the effects human activity has on the environment. A thorough exploration of the subject must address both of these aspects of the field because one cannot understand the *changes* that take place in the environment without first appreciating the environment's fundamental characteristics.

In the limited space available here, we have chosen to focus on the nature of pollution, its sources, its effects on the biotic and abiotic environment, and methods for controlling those effects. This approach seems appropriate because students are likely to be more familiar and more interested in such issues than in the general topic of the chemistry of the natural environment. To broaden students' understanding of more general topics in the field, the teacher is encouraged to become more familiar with and to make use of some of the books and Internet web sites listed in Appendix III.

This book can be used as a supplementary text in a beginning course. You can use specific sections of the text to illustrate concepts you are developing in the classroom, and/or as a source for special assignments, extra credit projects, or motivating devices. The text assumes that students have a basic background in chemistry, as well as limited experience with quantitative problem solving, organic chemistry, and other more advanced topics that may not be covered in introductory chemistry. Teachers may find it necessary to provide background information on topics that are unfamiliar to their students.

The text may also be used as the basis for an advanced course in environmental chemistry. In this case, we recommend that you supplement this text with other texts, references, and Internet sources.

Each chapter concludes with Exploration Activities. These are straightforward exercises that reinforce the basic principles presented in the chapter. The Answer Key is in Appendix II.

Appendix I has Additional Activities designed to be more challenging for students, calling for original research, creative thinking, and use of the Internet and other resources.

The author wishes to thank Professor Don Cass, College of the Atlantic, Bar Harbor, Maine, who read and commented on the first edition of this book. Professor Cass made many helpful comments and suggestions that enhanced the potential value of this book. Any errors that remain in the Second Edition are, however, entirely the responsibility of the author who, as always, appreciates receiving suggestions for changes and improvements in the text.

To the Student

Chemistry! Ugh! I hate the subject. It's all about moles and atomic orbitals and reaction rates. What does it have to do with the real world?

Perhaps you've heard other students make such comments about an introductory chemistry class. These comments may even have passed through your own mind.

But chemistry has many important applications to everyday life. Sometimes those applications do not become obvious until some time—perhaps much too long—after one has begun a study of the subject. But one has only to look through the daily newspaper or watch the evening news to realize the essential role chemistry has in daily events.

The purpose of this book is to show the relevance of chemistry to one very important field: environmental science, the study of human effects on the physical and biological environment. This text illustrates that understanding chemical principles can help you understand environmental changes and how the most harmful of those changes can be controlled.

However, this is only an introduction to environmental chemistry, a large and complex subject. For students interested in the topic, more advanced books, courses, and web sites are available, some of which are listed in Appendix III at the end of this book. But for now, let's begin at the beginning, with an overview of Earth, its environment, and the field of environmental chemistry.

BACKGROUND

Environmental Chemistry

TANKER LEAK ENDANGERS SEA LIFE

World Temperatures Reach Historic Highs

Hormones, Drugs Found in Public Water Supply

Green's Beach Closed after Sewage Spill

Report Says Toxic Wastes Are Draining from City Dump Sites

Headlines like these are common throughout the world today. They describe a range of environmental problems humans face in the modern world. Scientists from every discipline are looking for ways to deal with these problems.

Chemists are now—and have long been—involved in such problems. On one hand, the work that chemists do and the new products they invent often contribute to environmental degradation. The chemical genius that has produced countless varieties of plastics, for example, has inadvertently contributed to the problem of solid-waste disposal. The invention of exciting new compounds for the electronics industry has revolutionized communications, banking, transportation, and many other parts of our lives. But the by-products of those inventions account for a large percentage of the hazardous materials that contaminate the environment. Similar examples can be found in nearly every field of chemical research.

On the other hand, many problems *resulting* from chemical research may also be *solved* by chemical research. Chemists who invent plastics can also invent **biodegradable** plastics or plastics that are easier to recycle to reduce the use of petroleum in the production of new plastic. Researchers whose discoveries lead to dangerous by-products can also find ways of neutralizing those by-products. Finding ways to solve the world's environmental problems is as challenging and as exciting as the research that produces those problems.

> **Many problems resulting from chemical research may also be solved by chemical research.**

> **Environmental chemistry is the study of chemical phenomena in the environment.**

Research on natural and synthetic compounds in air, soil, and water has now become a specialized field of study, **environmental chemistry.** Environmental chemistry is the study of chemical phenomena in the environment. Included in this definition are problems such as the following:

1. What chemical species (elements, compounds, ions, free radicals, etc.) occur in the environment naturally?

2. Where do these species come from?

3. How are chemicals transported from one place to another in the environment?

4. What is the ultimate fate of chemicals in the environment?

5. What chemical reactions typically occur in the environment?

6. How do human activities influence chemical species and the reactions that occur among them in the environment?

 **Exploration Activities**

1. Define environmental chemistry.

2. What are some questions environmental chemists try to answer?

BACKGROUND

The Parts of the Earth

As a matter of convenience, scientists often divide Earth's environment into four primary areas: atmosphere, lithosphere, hydrosphere, and biosphere (Figure 1). The **atmosphere** is the envelope of gases that surrounds the earth. It is further divided into regions called the troposphere, stratosphere, mesosphere, and thermosphere. The **lithosphere** is the rigid outer crust of rock that can easily be studied by scientists. It is about 80 kilometers (50 miles) thick. Although the term *lithosphere* essentially refers to the earth's crust, only the thin outer layer of the crust—soil—is normally of interest to environmental chemists.

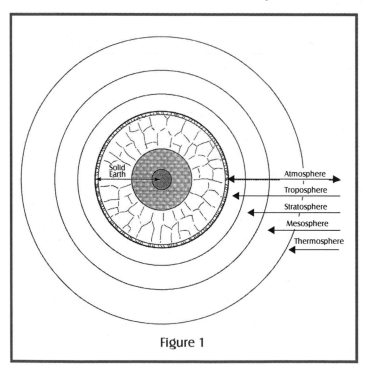

Figure 1

The **hydrosphere** is the watery portion of the planet, including its oceans, lakes, rivers, streams, groundwater, polar ice caps, glaciers, and other solid and liquid water resources. The hydrosphere covers nearly three quarters of the planet's surface.

The **biosphere** consists of all living organisms (including humans) on Earth. The lives of all organisms in the biosphere are influenced by their physical environment and, in turn, cause changes in the physical environment.

While this is true for all species, it is even more profoundly true for humans. The physical environment strongly influences the way humans can and do live. In turn, human societies alter other parts of the biosphere, the hydrosphere, the atmosphere, and the lithosphere, not only in their immediate living areas, but throughout the planet.

Some authorities have suggested adding a fifth sphere to this list, the **technosphere**. This term refers to the parts of our environment that humans produce, such as electronics, plastics, synthetic fibers, alloys, wood products, paper, and glass.

 **Exploration Activities**

1. Into what four regions do scientists often divide the earth?

2. Briefly describe each of the four regions.

BACKGROUND

Pure Resources

> **Even the most transparent stream in a remote mountain range contains many dissolved gases and minerals.**

Many scientists have addressed the subject of *pure* resources. People who are concerned about the environment, for example, often recommend that we maintain pure water supplies. The concept of pure resources is, however, somewhat abstract. Truly pure water contains nothing but water molecules. However, such a concept has little meaning in the real world. Water is a very efficient solvent. Even if a sample of pure water is stored in a clean glass container, a very tiny amount of glass from the container will, over time, dissolve in the water.

Water in the lithosphere is far from pure. Even the most transparent stream in a remote mountain range contains many dissolved gases and minerals. And, of course, water in the hydrosphere contains many dissolved substances.

The situation is even more complex with regard to pure air. Water is a compound. We can always imagine what a sample of pure water would be like. But air is a mixture. Its composition varies from place to place and from time to time. Creating a standard for a sample of pure air is virtually impossible.

The concept of pure water and air is not just an interesting academic debate. Resources that are thought to be pure by one group of people may be impure by another group's standards. Water and air may be pure enough for some purposes, but not for others. For example, when the U.S. Environmental Protection Agency (EPA) conducts its semiannual survey of water conditions in the United States, it classifies rivers, streams, lakes, and other bodies of water as safe for (1) the support of aquatic life, (2) consumption of fish, (3) primary contact, such as swimming, (4) secondary contact, such as boating, (5) as a source of drinking water, and (6) for use in agriculture.

Another aspect of the purity debate is that there are increasingly precise methods available for detecting the presence of impurities in water and air. The presence of a few parts per million of a substance dissolved in water or air was once considered precise. Now, detecting one part per trillion is not unusual. Is water impure if it contains 3 parts per trillion of some dissolved substance?

 **EXPLORE**   **Exploration Activities**

1. Can absolutely pure water be found on the earth? Explain.

2. Chemically, what is the major difference between air and water in the environment?

BACKGROUND

Contaminants and Pollutants

> **A contaminant is any material that normally is not present in some part of the environment but, when present, is harmless to humans and other organisms.**

Most people have a common understanding of the term *pure*. Often a resource is said to be pure if it is safe to drink, breathe, or eat. For example, a mountain stream that contains only dissolved gases and minerals that are harmless to humans is not pure from a strictly chemical standpoint. But many people would call it pure because the water is safe to drink.

The terms *contamination* and *pollution* are sometimes used to describe resources that are not pure. Scientists do not necessarily agree on how these terms should be used. Some authorities say the terms are synonymous. Other authorities make a distinction between the two concepts. The latter authorities would say that a **contaminant** is any material that normally is not present in some part of the environment but, when present, is harmless to humans and other organisms.

For example, a paper manufacturer discharges very small amounts of waste mercury into a clear mountain stream. The concentration of mercury is far less than the amount known to harm humans or other organisms. In this case, the waste mercury could be called a contaminant. However, the substance is considered a contaminant and not a pollutant only because such low concentrations exist in the stream. If larger amounts of mercury were discharged, they would soon reach dangerous levels. A contaminant, then, is a foreign substance that occurs at a low enough concentration in the environment not to harm living organisms.

Those who distinguish between a contaminant and a pollutant reserve the latter term for materials that actually pose a threat to humans and other organisms. For example, as the concentration of waste mercury in a stream increases, it becomes a pollutant. A **pollutant** is a material present in some part of the environment in a high enough concentration to cause harmful effects in organisms.

The difference between contaminants and pollutants also takes into consideration the organisms affected. For example, the fish in a stream contaminated with mercury might be more sensitive to this substance than the humans drinking the water. Thus, the stream can be said to be polluted when it contains materials that pose a threat to fish (or other organisms in the stream) even when those materials are not dangerous to humans.

EXPLORE   **Exploration Activities**

1. How does pollution differ from contamination?

2. Do you think it's important to make a distinction between a contaminant and a pollutant? Why or why not?

BACKGROUND

Natural Cleansing Processes

Contamination and pollution can be natural phenomena. For example, a forest fire pollutes the air with smoke. Pollution can also result from human activities. The air in many communities is polluted during the winter by smoke from wood-burning stoves in private homes. The term **anthropogenic** is used to describe substances and events that are caused by human activities. In the case of either natural or anthropogenic events, natural processes exist by which contaminants and pollutants are removed from the environment.

The most common of these processes is *dilution*. When a gas is released into the atmosphere or liquids are released into bodies of water, they are distributed throughout the entire volume of the substance into which they are released. As the concentration decreases, they tend to become less of a risk to humans, other animals, and plant life.

For example, smoke from campfires is moved about by winds and air currents. Gaseous products in the smoke, such as carbon dioxide and carbon monoxide, are eventually distributed throughout the whole atmosphere. Solid particles, such as ash, remain in the atmosphere for days, weeks, months, or even years. But these particles eventually settle back to the ground.

The final location in which a contaminant or pollutant is deposited for an extended period of time is called a **sink.** In this example, the whole atmosphere is a sink for the gases in campfire smoke.

However, no substance remains in a sink forever. For example, carbon dioxide from campfire smoke eventually becomes part of the carbon cycle. It is incorporated into minerals or living organisms. This reminds us that we can never really throw something away forever. Every waste material is eventually recycled into some part of the environment.

Thus, contamination and pollution are normal phenomena in the environment, resulting from both natural processes and human activities, and they are subject to removal by natural cleansing processes.

> **Contamination and pollution are subject to removal by natural cleansing processes.**

 **Exploration Activities**

1. What is an *anthropogenic* pollutant?

2. Explain the process of dilution.

3. What is a sink?

11

BACKGROUND

The History of Pollution

Pollution has been a problem—at least at some times and in some places—throughout all of human history. Imagine early cave or tent dwellers trying to cook their meals over a smoking fire. These early humans would have understood the concept of polluted air very well.

But for much of human history, such examples were relatively rare. Most people lived simple lives, and the few waste products they released to the environment were quickly distributed throughout the environment. In addition, those waste products were usually natural materials, such as wood, bones, and clay, that were found in the environment anyway or that decayed rapidly and harmlessly.

Dramatic increases in population and the development of modern chemical technology exploded the effects humans have on their environment. First, people began to congregate into large, more densely packed communities. The earliest cities contained only a few tens or hundreds of thousands of people. But even in such relatively small cities, pollution could become a problem. Without sophisticated methods of waste disposal, agricultural and human wastes, spoiled food, dead plants and animals, and other waste products could collect in rivers and lakes, creating conditions under which disease-causing organisms could proliferate.

One of the earliest documented environmental laws was promulgated in 1306 by King Edward I of England. The law stated that "whosoever shall be found guilty of burning coal shall suffer the loss of his head." This law became necessary because the densely packed population of London depended on the burning of soft coal for heating and cooking. The soft coal then available was a very inefficient fuel, producing huge quantities of suffocating black smoke that often became trapped by the city's naturally cloudy environment.

An important development in the history of environmental chemistry was when researchers began to realize that polluted air and water are not just unpleasant and inconvenient, but that they actually represent a threat to human health (as well as the health of other animals and plants). One of the most famous examples of this

> **One of the earliest documented environmental laws was promulgated in 1306.**

understanding came in 1853 during a cholera epidemic in London. A physician by the name of John Snow realized that most of the cholera victims were using a common source for their water, a pump located on Broad Street. Snow's recommendation for ending the epidemic was to "remove the pump handle," forcing people to find another source of water. It was later discovered that the well over which the Broad Street pump was located was being contaminated by wastes draining out of a tenement building where a person with cholera had been living.

The rise of modern chemical technology in the late eighteenth century was the second major change leading to the rise of modern pollution. For the first time in history, humans learned how to manipulate materials to produce a host of synthetic new products, such as alloys, dyes, medicines, and artificial fibers, with huge and unimagined benefits for humankind. Unfortunately, these new products brought correspondingly profound and unexpected risks to the biological and physical environment.

Many of these new risks and benefits became obvious with the development of the young steel industry in the mid-1800s. With the English inventor Henry Bessemer's (1813-98) invention of an inexpensive method for making good steel, a whole host of new industries and products became possible, including bridges, railways, tall buildings, and oceangoing ships.

But the clouds of suffocating black smoke that spread over the English countryside as a result of Bessemer's invention and the industries it spawned were a considerable price to pay for the progress they brought. People soon realized that they were faced with a difficult trade-off: They could have that progress, with more jobs, more profits, better wages, and an improved lifestyle (for some people), but only at the expense of a more polluted and more dangerous environment. Added to that equation was the fact that those who gained the least (the workers) were likely to suffer the most from the trade-off, since they were most likely to live in the densely populated, polluted cities that housed the factories. And those who gained the most (the owners) were likely to avoid the worst consequences of the trade-off, since they could afford to live outside of the polluted cities.

That dilemma exists today. Communities often have the opportunity to invite new industries to settle in their area, with the promise of

> **Clouds of suffocating black smoke were a considerable price to pay for the progress they brought.**

How do we find balance between economic development and environmental protection?

new jobs, increased tax revenue, and other economic benefits to the community. But in many cases, those industries are likely to have a negative impact on the environment, possibly increasing air and water pollution. So the community has a choice: welcome a potentially polluting industry and improve the economic climate, or reject the industry and maintain the quality of the environment, at the cost of jobs and increased tax revenues.

Thus, when members of the U.S. Senate in the early twenty-first-century debate on President George W. Bush's plan for drilling for oil in the primitive wilderness of the Arctic National Wildlife Refuge, they are only replaying a debate that has continued for more than two centuries: How do we find the balance between the values of economic development and the values of environmental protection?

Exploration Activities

1. What two factors account for the increase in pollution around the world in the last century?

2. In what respects can pollution be considered to be both a benefit and a risk for human societies and the environment?

walch.com   15

BACKGROUND

Introduction

Throughout history, one of the most obvious examples of environmental contamination has been air pollution. Recall the edict of King Edward I restricting the burning of soft coal because of the offensive clouds of smoke it produced. One of the major factors leading to the rise of the modern environmental movement in the 1960s was the rapid increase in urban smog conditions, such as those experienced in Los Angeles. It was not easy to ignore pollution problems when people could not walk down a street without seeing an ugly brown haze everywhere that made them cough and caused their eyes to sting.

But air pollution problems are not confined to such obvious visual and respiratory effects in urban areas. Today, pollutants can be detected in virtually every part of the world, including the deserts and the polar ice caps. And visible contaminants make up only a fraction of all those that exist today. Carbon monoxide, for example, is one of the most deadly of all atmospheric contaminants. Yet, it is invisible to the naked eye.

Understanding the mechanics and effects of air pollution is a complex scientific challenge. Earth's atmosphere is a complicated, active machine of which pollutants have become a relatively small but crucial part. This chapter provides a general introduction to the physical and chemical characteristics of the atmosphere. Environmental problems occurring within the atmosphere are described briefly here and then discussed in more detail later in the book.

Today, pollutants can be detected in virtually every part of the world.

BACKGROUND

Structure of the Atmosphere

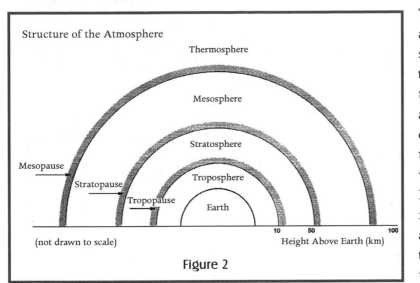

Structure of the Atmosphere

Figure 2

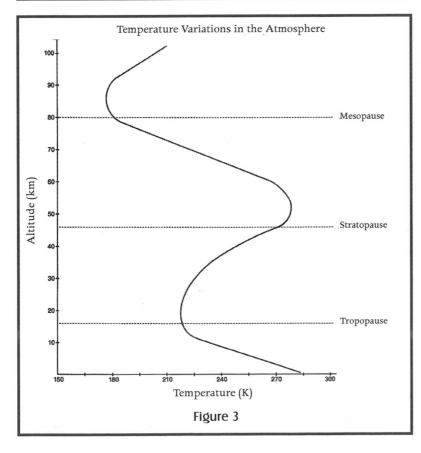

Temperature Variations in the Atmosphere

Figure 3

The vast majority of human activity takes place in the lowest shell of the atmosphere, the **troposphere.** As Figure 2 shows, the troposphere extends to a height of about 10–16 kilometers above the earth's surface. Temperatures in the troposphere correspond to those with which we are familiar on Earth, ranging from about 20°C near the earth's surface to approximately –60°C at the **tropopause,** the upper limit of the troposphere.

Figure 3 shows how temperatures change from the earth's surface, through the troposphere and into the upper levels of the atmosphere. Notice that the temperature falls at a fairly regular rate within the troposphere, about 9.8°C/km. This temperature decrease is known as the **tropospheric lapse rate.**

The next layer of the atmosphere, the **stratosphere,** extends from the tropopause upward to a height of about 50 kilometers. Very little human activity occurs within the stratosphere. One exception is the high-flying jet airplanes that travel in this region. Still, physical and chemical changes in the stratosphere can have profound effects on life on Earth. In turn, human activities can effect changes in the chemical composition of the stratosphere. The nature of those changes is described later in the book.

Possibly the most interesting chemical species within the stratosphere is ozone, O_3, an *allotrope* of oxygen. Ozone molecules absorb energy in the ultraviolet region of the electromagnetic spectrum. Thus, some portion of ultraviolet radiation from the Sun is captured in the stratosphere. This absorption of energy accounts for a rise in temperature from about $-60°C$ at the tropopause to nearly $0°C$ at the **stratopause,** the top of the stratosphere.

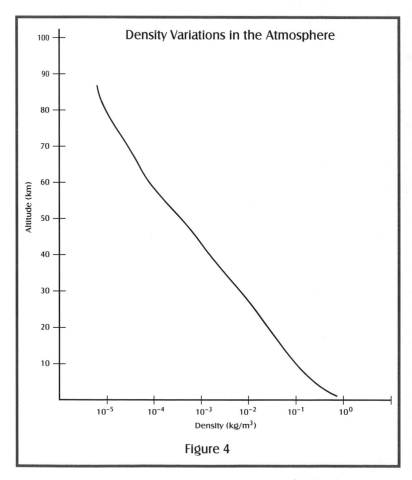

Density Variations in the Atmosphere

Figure 4

The layer above the stratosphere is the **mesosphere.** Gravitational attraction in the upper regions of the atmosphere, including the mesosphere, is quite weak. Molecules have a tendency to escape from these regions entirely. The density of gases above the stratosphere is very low, less then $10^{-5}kg/m^3$. Figure 4 shows how density drops off from the earth's surface to the top of the atmosphere.

Two less familiar chemical species that occur in the mesosphere are the ions O_2^+ and NO^+. Neither of these species absorbs much solar radiation. Thus, the temperature within the mesosphere falls from about $0°C$ at the stratopause to nearly $-100°C$ at its upper boundary, about 85 km above the earth's surface.

In the **thermosphere,** the atmosphere's uppermost layer, temperatures rise from about $-100°C$ to more than $1,000°C$ at the atmosphere's outermost limits. This temperature measures the average kinetic energy of molecules present in the thermosphere. Since this energy is large, the temperature in the region is high. Recall, however, that the density of gases in the thermosphere is very low. Thus, the amount of heat in this region of the atmosphere is also very low. In addition to O_2^+ and NO^+, the singly charged oxygen ion O^+ also occurs.

EXPLORE   Exploration Activities

1. Name the four layers of the atmosphere.

2. In what layer of the atmosphere would you find ozone? What purpose does it serve?

BACKGROUND

Composition of the Troposphere

The most abundant chemicals in the troposphere are nitrogen, oxygen, argon, carbon dioxide, and water. Table 1 lists the major components of dry tropospheric air at sea level. Since air is a mixture, this composition may vary from place to place and from time to time. The concentration of water vapor, in particular, varies widely from place to place.

> **The concentration of gases produced by organic decay is very low.**

MAJOR COMPONENTS OF DRY TROPOSPHERIC AIR AT SEA LEVEL	
Component	**Concentration (percent by volume)**
nitrogen	78.084
oxygen	20.948
argon	0.934
carbon dioxide	0.0371*

*Fluctuates as a result of human activities; 2001 estimate
Table 1

In addition to the major components listed in Table 1, tropospheric air contains a number of other minor components. Table 2 lists some of these components. Some of the substances listed in the table are the product of natural changes taking place on Earth. Perhaps the most common of these changes is the decay of organic material. This decay typically produces methane (CH_4), nitrous oxide (N_2O), ammonia (NH_3), carbon disulfide (CS_2), carbonyl sulfide (COS), and other trace gases.

The concentration of gases produced by organic decay is very low. Typically, the concentration of methane and nitrous oxide, the most abundant gases produced by this process, is of the order of 10^{-5}–10^{-4} parts per million by volume, or ppmv (nitrous oxide is also produced by mechanisms other than organic decay). In certain regions, these concentrations may be significantly higher. Animals kept in **feedlots,** for example, often produce huge volumes of manure, the decay of which may result in unusually high levels of methane, nitrous oxide, and other gases in the surrounding air.

Hydrogen sulfide (H_2S) and sulfur dioxide (SO_2) are also present in the atmosphere. Both gases are released during volcanic action, at hot springs, and during the eruption of geysers. Salt crystals produced during the evaporation of ocean spray are yet another chemical species found in tropospheric air.

MINOR COMPONENTS OF DRY TROPOSPHERIC AIR AT SEA LEVEL*	
Component	Concentration (parts per million by volume)
neon	18.0
helium	5.2
methane	1.65
krypton	1.1
hydrogen	0.58
nitrous oxide	0.33
xenon	0.09
ozone	0.01–0.1
carbon monoxide	0.01
nitric oxide and nitrogen dioxide	10^{-6}–10^{-2}
ammonia	10^{-4}–10^{-3}
sulfur dioxide	10^{-5}–10^{-4}
nitric acid	10^{-5}–10^{-3}

*Different authorities cite different values for the concentrations of these species. The values given here are those provided by J. H. Seinfeld, *Atmospheric Chemistry and Physics of Air Pollution* (New York: Wiley, 1986) and P. Brimblecombe, *Air Composition and Chemistry* (Cambridge, England: Cambridge University Press, 1986).

Table 2

EXPLORE   **Exploration Activities**

1. What are the most abundant gases produced by organic decay? What other processes produce these gases in larger volumes?

2. What other natural processes produce components of the troposphere?

22

BACKGROUND

Anthropogenic Components

Human activities also release many different chemical species into the atmosphere. Every industrial process, for example, results in the release of chemicals. The most significant human source of atmospheric contamination is the combustion of fossil fuels.

The term **fossil fuel** refers to coal, oil, and natural gas. Most scientists believe that these fuels were produced millions of years ago, probably as a result of the decay of plants, animals, and other organic matter. The production of the fossil fuels appears to have been essentially a one-time phenomenon. That is, the earth's current store of coal, oil, and natural gas is probably limited to the amounts produced some 300 million years ago. We have no evidence that fossil fuels are being created now, nor have they been for millions of years. They are, therefore, **nonrenewable resources.** When they have been extracted and used up, they will probably be gone for at least the foreseeable future, if not forever.

Coal, oil, and natural gas are all complex mixtures. Natural gas is perhaps the simplest of the three. It consists primarily (about 85%) of methane (CH_4). Another 10% consists of ethane (C_2H_6). Propane (C_3H_8), butane (C_4H_{10}), and nitrogen (N) make up the remaining 5% of natural gas.

The main component of coal is elemental carbon (C). The percentage of carbon in coal varies depending on the type of coal, as shown in Table 3. Solid, liquid, and gaseous hydrocarbons, along with small amounts of inorganic compounds, make up the fraction of coal not accounted for by carbon. In

TYPICAL COMPOSITION OF VARIOUS TYPES OF COAL				
Form	Carbon	Volatile Matter	Moisture	Ash
peat	—	about 20%	about 80%	—
lignite	30%	28%	37%	5%
sub-bituminous (soft coal)	40%	32%	19%	9%
bituminous (soft coal)	45–65%	20–45%	2–5%	5–10%
anthracite (hard coal)	82%	5%	4%	9%

Table 3

terms of its environmental impact, the most significant trace element in coal is usually sulfur. Various types of coal may contain anywhere from less than 1% to more than 5% sulfur.

Petroleum is a highly complex mixture of solid, liquid, and gaseous hydrocarbons. It also contains small amounts of inorganic compounds. Any sample of petroleum may consist of hundreds of different compounds. The complex nature of petroleum makes it largely unusable for commercial purposes. To make it an economically useful product, it is first refined, or separated, into somewhat simpler fractions. Figure 5 shows how petroleum is separated in a fractionating tower. The numbered boxes describe the steps that occur in the fractionating process.

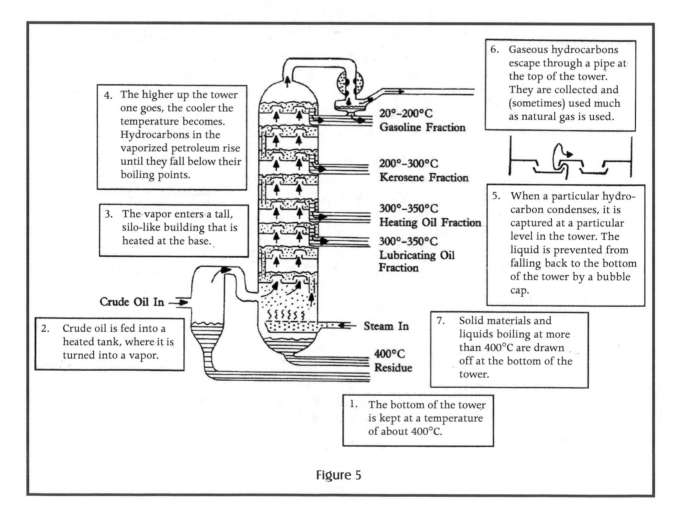

4. The higher up the tower one goes, the cooler the temperature becomes. Hydrocarbons in the vaporized petroleum rise until they fall below their boiling points.

3. The vapor enters a tall, silo-like building that is heated at the base.

Crude Oil In →

2. Crude oil is fed into a heated tank, where it is turned into a vapor.

20°–200°C Gasoline Fraction

200°–300°C Kerosene Fraction

300°–350°C Heating Oil Fraction

300°–350°C Lubricating Oil Fraction

Steam In

400°C Residue

6. Gaseous hydrocarbons escape through a pipe at the top of the tower. They are collected and (sometimes) used much as natural gas is used.

5. When a particular hydrocarbon condenses, it is captured at a particular level in the tower. The liquid is prevented from falling back to the bottom of the tower by a bubble cap.

7. Solid materials and liquids boiling at more than 400°C are drawn off at the bottom of the tower.

1. The bottom of the tower is kept at a temperature of about 400°C.

Figure 5

Exploration Activities

1. To what does the term *fossil fuel* refer?

2. How do various forms of coal differ from one another?

3. Why is petroleum refined?

BACKGROUND

Combustion of Fossil Fuels

Since the Industrial Revolution, humans have been using coal, oil, and natural gas to power machinery, heat homes and buildings, carry out chemical processes in industry, and power all forms of transportation. The vast majority of these applications depends on a single chemical reaction, the combustion of organic compounds known as hydrocarbons.

Consider, as an example, the combustion of pure methane gas. In the presence of excess oxygen and at high temperatures, methane oxidizes completely to yield carbon dioxide and water as products:

$$CH_4(g) + 2O_2(g) \rightarrow CO_2(g) + 2H_2O(g)$$

A similar reaction occurs with any fossil fuel. The octane in petroleum, for examples, oxidizes completely to yield carbon dioxide and water:

$$2C_8H_{18}(l) + 25O_2(g) \rightarrow 16CO_2(g) + 18H_2O(g)$$

The products of the complete combustion of organic compounds, CO_2 and H_2O, are both naturally occurring compounds that normally pose no threat to the environment. However, normal circumstances have been altered in recent decades. The amount of fossil fuels burned has increased so dramatically that enormous quantities of carbon dioxide have been released into the atmosphere. Some scientists now worry that this increase in atmospheric carbon dioxide may have long-term harmful effects on our environment. A more detailed analysis of this *greenhouse effect* is presented later in the book.

Incomplete Combustion of Fossil Fuels

The complete combustion of fossil fuels rarely occurs in the real world. Incomplete combustion occurs when temperatures are too low and/or oxygen is not provided to the fuel rapidly enough to allow all fuel molecules to reach their highest possible state of oxidation. Instead, those fuel molecules escape in a partially oxidized state or even in their original, unreacted form.

26

Consider again the oxidation of methane gas, this time in a real-world situation. Partial oxidation of a sample of methane results in the formation of water vapor, carbon dioxide, carbon monoxide (CO), and elemental carbon (C). In addition, some unburned methane escapes from the reaction mixture.

$$CH_4(g) + O_2(g) \rightarrow CO_2(g) + H_2O(g) + CO(g) + C(s) + CH_4(g)$$

No attempt should be made to balance this equation since it does not represent a *stoichiometric reaction*. That is, different products in different ratios are formed each time the reaction occurs. So no single, balanced equation can represent all the different reactions that occur.

Incomplete combustion of octane and other organic compounds produces comparable results. The hydrocarbon (HC) term in the following equation represents unburned hydrocarbons released during combustion.

$$C_8H_{18}(l) + O_2(g) \rightarrow CO_2(g) + H_2O(g) + CO(g) + C(s) + HC$$

Some of the compounds represented by the HC term in equations like this one include methane, ethane, propane, butane, pentane, benzene, toluene, ethylbenzene, ethene, propene, isoprene, cyclopentane, cyclopentene, and acetylene. The nature of hydrocarbons in fossil fuels is discussed in more detail later in the book.

The products of the incomplete combustion of fossil fuels are major constituents of polluted air. Carbon monoxide is responsible for a variety of human health problems, while finely divided carbon (as soot or **particulates**) accounts for some of the hazy appearance of polluted skies and the sooty fallout that covers some industrial areas. Unburned hydrocarbons react with other chemical species in the atmosphere to produce a complex mixture of products that make up **photochemical smog.** The causes, nature, and treatment of air pollutants such as these are also discussed later on.

The Combustion of Trace Elements in Fossil Fuels

By far the most important trace element in fossil fuels is sulfur. Sulfur may occur in an elemental form, although it more commonly occurs in the form of organic and/or inorganic compounds. During the combustion of coal, oil, and natural gas, sulfur is oxidized to sulfur dioxide (SO_2).

$$S(s) + O_2(g) \rightarrow SO_2(g)$$

A small fraction of the sulfur is oxidized directly to the +6 oxidation state as sulfur trioxide (SO_3).

$$2S(s) + 3O_2(g) \rightarrow 2SO_3(g)$$

The majority of SO_2 produced during fossil fuel combustion is converted in the atmosphere to SO_3.

$$2SO_2(g) + O_2(g) \rightarrow 2SO_3$$

Fossil fuels may also contain small amounts of nitrogen compounds. These nitrogen compounds are normally oxidized to nitric oxide (NO), which, in turn, may be converted to nitrogen dioxide (NO_2).

$$2N \text{ (in compounds)} + O_2(g) \rightarrow 2NO(g)$$

$$2NO(g) + O_2(g) \rightarrow 2NO_2(g)$$

A more important source of these two nitrogen oxides, however, is the reaction between elemental nitrogen and oxygen in the atmosphere. At ambient temperatures, nitrogen and oxygen are essentially unreactive. But an increase in temperature increases the rate at which NO is formed from the elements. The equilibrium concentration of NO also increases. At 27°C, for example, the concentration of NO in air is 1.1×10^{-10} ppmv. At 527°C, that concentration rises to 0.77 ppmv; and at 1,316°C, to 550 ppm. Figure 6 shows the relationship between temperature and NO concentration up to the normal temperature range of some internal combustion engines.

Figure 6

Concentration of NO at Various Temperatures*

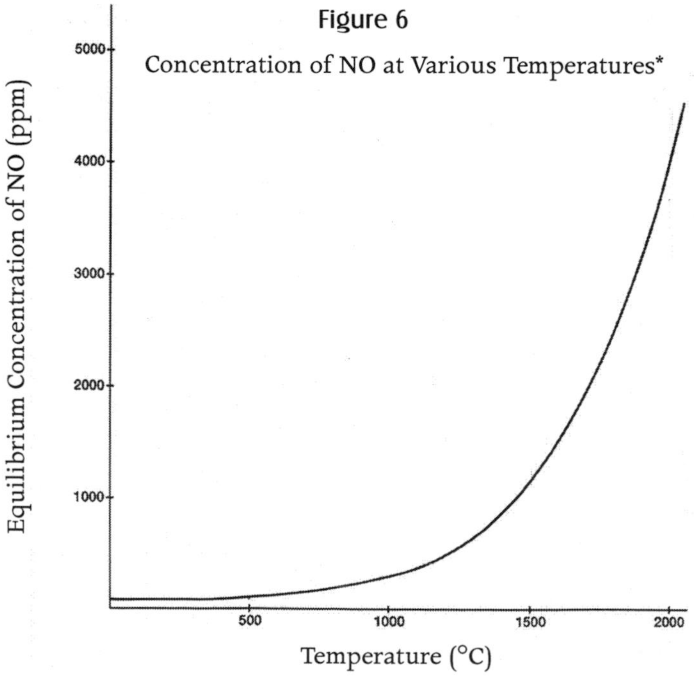

Y-axis: Equilibrium Concentration of NO (ppm)

X-axis: Temperature (°C)

* Data from U.S. Department of Health, Education, and Welfare, *Control Techniques for Nitrogen Oxide Emissions from Stationary Sources,* March 1970, p. 3–1.

The formulas NO_x and, less commonly, SO_x are used to represent the oxides of nitrogen and sulfur. Like CO and particulates, the oxides of nitrogen and sulfur are important components of polluted air.

Component	Range of Composition (in percent)
Si (as SiO_2)	17.3–63.6
Al (as Al_2O_3)	9.8–58.4
K (as K_2O_3)	2.8–3.0
Fe (as Fe_2O_3 or Fe_3O_4)	2.0–26.8
C (as C)	0.37–36.2
Na (as Na_2O)	0.2–0.9
S (as SO_3)	0.12–24.33
Ca (as CaO)	0.12–14.33
Mg (as MgO)	0.06–4.77
P (as P)	0.03–20.6
Ti (as TiO_2)	0.0–2.8

COMPOSITION OF FLY ASH*

*As reported in W. S. Smith and C. W. Gruber, *Atmospheric Emissions from Coal Combustion: An Inventory Guide* (Cincinnati: U.S. Department of Health, Education, and Welfare, Division of Air Pollution, 1966).

Table 4

Fly Ash

Coal normally contains small amounts of many different inorganic compounds. When coal burns, these compounds are converted to oxides that escape as **fly ash.** Fly ash is a finely divided solid produced during coal combustion. The composition of fly ash differs considerably depending on the type of coal burned. Table 4 shows the type and concentration of products found in a typical sample of fly ash.

The vast majority of fly ash particles are very small, about 1 μm in diameter. The minute size of these particles means that they are able to enter the respiratory system of animals easily. Also, their small size makes their removal from waste gases especially difficult.

Exploration Activities

1. What are the two most abundant products of the complete combustion of any fossil fuel?

2. What are the products of the incomplete combustion of any fossil fuel?

3. What is the most significant anthropogenic source of SO_2 in the atmosphere?

4. How does human activity tend to increase the concentration of NO_x in the atmosphere?

BACKGROUND   # Types of Pollutants

In summary, air pollutants can be classified into one of seven general categories. These categories are:

1. Carbon monoxide (CO)

2. Sulfur dioxide (SO_2) and sulfur trioxide (SO_3)

3. Nitrogen oxides (NO_x)

4. Hydrocarbons (HC)

5. Photochemical oxidants

6. Particulate matter

7. Other elements and compounds, such as ozone, asbestos, heavy metals, ammonia, hydrogen sulfide (H_2S), sulfuric and nitric acids (H_2SO_4 and HNO_3), and radioactive materials.

AMOUNTS AND SOURCES OF FIVE MAJOR AIR POLLUTANTS* (in millions of metric tons)					
Source	CO	Particulates	NO_x	SO_2	Volatile Organics
Transportation	63.76	1.20	11.83	1.28	7.06
Stationary fuel combustion	4.87	1.71	9.24	15.16	0.81
Industrial processes	3.38	1.21	0.72	1.32	7.27
Solid wastes	1.05	0.50	0.09	0.03	0.39
Miscellaneous	8.09	29.17	0.30	0.01	0.70
Total	81.15	33.79	22.18	17.80	16.23
Ranking according to amount produced	1	2	3	4	5
Estimate ranking according to health effect	5	2	4	1	3

*Adapted from National Air Pollution Emission Trends, 1900–1998, March 2000, Environmental Protection Agency, www.epa.gov/ttn/chief/trends98

Table 5

All of the pollutants listed above except photochemical oxidants are **primary pollutants,** substances that are released directly into the atmosphere as the result of some human activity. Photochemical oxidants are an example of **secondary pollutants,** substances that are formed in the environment as the result of chemical reactions among primary pollutants and naturally occurring substances.

Table 5 on the previous page summarizes the most recent data available on the amounts of five major pollutants released to the atmosphere each year in the United States and the source of each pollutant. The table also shows the relative importance of each pollutant as a threat to the environment. Notice that the pollutant appearing in the largest amount is not necessarily regarded by experts as the most serious threat. Carbon monoxide ranks number one in terms of annual emissions, but most authorities do not classify it as the primary threat to the environment.

Exploration Activities

1. List the seven general categories of air pollutants.

2. Explain how a primary pollutant differs from a secondary pollutant.

BACKGROUND

Air Quality Standards

In the United States, Canada, the United Kingdom, and other developed nations, modern regulation of air quality dates only to the 1960s. One of the earliest forms of legislation adopted in the United States was the Clean Air Act of 1965. That act focused on problems of air pollution created by motor vehicles. It set standards for the maximum amounts of carbon monoxide and hydrocarbons that could be emitted from cars, trucks, and other forms of transportation. Five years later, a more stringent set of standards was created in the Clean Air Act of 1970, actually a set of amendments to the legislation adopted in 1965. The 1970 act established new standards for air quality, set new limits on emissions from stationary and mobile sources, and increased funds for air pollution research.

NATIONAL AMBIENT AIR QUALITY STANDARDS (NAAQS), 1990

Pollutant	Maximum Recommended Concentration	
	Primary Standard	Secondary Standard
Carbon monoxide 8 hour average 1 hour average	9 ppm (10 mg/m^3) 35 ppm (40 mg/m^3)	none 35 ppm (40 mg/m^3)
Nitrogen dioxide 1 year average	0.053 ppm (100 µg/m^3)	0.053 ppm (100 µg/m^3)
Ozone 8 hour average 1 hour average	0.08 ppm (157 µg/m^3) 0.12 ppm (235 µg/m^3)	0.08 ppm (157 µg/m^3) 0.12 ppm (235 µg/m^3)
Lead 3 month average	1.5 µg/m^3	1.5 µg/m^3
Sulfur dioxide 3 hour average 24 hour average 1 year average	none 0.14 ppm 0.03 ppm	0.50 ppm none none
Particulates (PM 2.5)* 24 hour average 1 year average	65 µg/m^3 15.0 Mg/m^3	65 µg/m^3 15.0 Mg/m^3
Particulates (PM 10)* 24 hour average 1 year average	150 µg/m^3 50 µg/m^3	150 µg/m^3 50 µg/m^3

*EPA sets separate standards for particulate matter consisting of particles 2.5 µg or less in diameter (PM 2.5) and for particles between 2.5 and 10 µg. For further information, see the EPA web site on National Ambient Air Quality Standards at www.epa.gov/airs/criteria.html.

Table 6

Air quality standards were further developed by additional amendments to the Clean Air Act adopted in 1990.

One provision of the Clean Air Act is a requirement that the U.S. Environmental Protection Agency (EPA) establish, publish, and enforce a set of standards for six major "criteria pollutants": carbon monoxide, sulfur dioxide, nitrogen dioxide, ozone, lead, and two kinds of particulates. Table 6 summarizes the EPA's most recent listing of air quality standards. Notice that two levels of standards are provided. The **primary standards** are more restrictive. They are designed to protect the health of all humans. The EPA sets these standards high enough to ensure protection of those who are especially sensitive to pollutants: young children, the elderly, and those with respiratory disorders. **Secondary standards** are less restrictive. They are intended to provide protection to animals, crops, buildings, and other nonhuman elements in the environment. Notice that three units of measure are used in Table 6, milligrams per cubic meter of air (mg/m^3), micrograms per cubic meter of air (μg/m^3), and parts per million (ppm).

EXPLORE   **Exploration Activities**

1. When the Clean Air Act was first adopted in the United States in 1965, what problems did it address?

2. How do primary air standards differ from secondary standards?

BACKGROUND

Sources of Pollutants

Most compounds classified as air pollutants also occur naturally in the atmosphere. Carbon monoxide, for example, is formed naturally by the oxidation of methane in the atmosphere. Nitrogen oxides are formed when lightning catalyzes the combination of elemental nitrogen and oxygen.

$$2CH_4(g) + 3O_2(g) \rightarrow 2CO(g) + 4H_2O(l)$$

$$N_2(g) + O_2(g) \rightarrow 2NO(g)$$

In fact, as Table 7 shows, the anthropogenic contribution of four major pollutants is actually relatively small.

NATURAL AND ANTHROPOGENIC SOURCES OF MAJOR POLLUTANTS*		
Pollutant	**Approximate Fraction From**	
	Natural Sources	**Anthropogenic Sources**
Carbon monoxide	91%	9%
Sulfur oxides	55%	45%
Nitrogen oxides	89%	11%
Hydrocarbons	84%	16%
Particulates	89%	11%

*As cited in H. Stephen Stoker and Spencer L. Seager, *Environmental Chemistry*, Second Edition (Glenview, IL: Scott Foresman, 1976), pp. 10, 32, 48, 67, & 86.

Table 7

The table illustrates the obvious problems sulfur dioxide poses. Human activities roughly double the concentration of this pollutant in the atmosphere. The danger posed by the anthropogenic release of the other pollutants is more serious than the raw numbers in Table 7 would indicate. Naturally occurring CO, NOx, particulates, and hydrocarbons are distributed rather uniformly worldwide. Their concentration in any one location as a result of natural factors is unlikely to pose a threat to the environment or to humans. By comparison, CO, NOx, particulates, and hydrocarbons released by human activities tend to be concentrated in specific locations, such as industrial or crowded urban areas. This concentration greatly magnifies the health risk posed by the pollutants.

 **EXPLORE** **Exploration Activity**

Why is the anthropogenic contribution of pollutants so harmful? Explain.

BACKGROUND

Carbon Monoxide

Three of the six major air pollutants—carbon monoxide, sulfur dioxide, and the oxides of nitrogen—are nonmetallic oxides. These oxides are produced by natural sources, such as the decay of organic material and volcanic action, and as the result of human activities. This chapter describes the sources and ultimate fates of these materials, their potential effects on plants and animals (including humans), and methods available for their control.

Carbon monoxide (CO) is formed as a result of the incomplete oxidation of carbon-containing materials. This process occurs during both natural and anthropogenic changes. The average worldwide atmospheric concentration of carbon monoxide is estimated to be about 0.1 ppm.

> **Carbon monoxide is formed as a result of the incomplete oxidation of carbon-containing materials.**

Sources and Sinks

The most common natural source of carbon monoxide in the atmosphere is the oxidation of methane, a process that occurs in a complex series of reactions. That series of reactions begins when methane (CH_4) reacts with the hydroxyl radical ($OH \cdot$) and is then converted sequentially to the methyl radical ($CH_3 \cdot$), the methoxy radical ($CH_3O_2 \cdot$), formaldehyde (HCHO), the formyl radical ($HCO \cdot$), and finally, carbon monoxide:

$$CH_4 + OH \cdot \rightarrow CH_3 \cdot \rightarrow CH_3O_2 \cdot \rightarrow HCHO \rightarrow HCO \cdot \rightarrow CO$$

The net change that occurs as a result of these reactions can be summarized by the following equation:

$$2CH_4(g) + 3O_2(g) \rightarrow 2CO(g) + 4H_2O(g)$$

Carbon monoxide is also produced directly and in smaller amounts by living green plants that are exposed to sunlight, from dead and decaying plant matter, from the soil and wetlands, from rice paddies, and from bacteria, algae, jellyfish, and other organisms that live in the oceans. The total amount of carbon monoxide in the atmosphere has been estimated at about 2.780×10^9 kg, about half of which is produced naturally, and about half (1.350×10^9 kg) through anthropogenic processes.

Naturally occurring carbon monoxide is generally not regarded as an environmental problem because it is distributed so widely at very low concentrations throughout the earth's atmosphere. If anthropogenic carbon monoxide were also distributed equally throughout the air, it would pose few health risks. The problem is that the carbon monoxide from anthropogenic sources tends to accumulate in high concentrations in certain geographic locations, such as urban areas. Researchers have measured concentrations of 115 ppm inside vehicles during rush hour at busy downtown intersections, which is far in excess of those considered safe for humans. In such cases, the level of carbon monoxide to which humans and other organisms are exposed may be enough to pose a significant health hazard.

The high concentration of carbon monoxide in heavily populated areas is a result of the combustion of fossil fuels in transportation and industry. The personal automobile is the single most important anthropogenic source of the compound.

Natural processes appear to be highly efficient in removing carbon monoxide from the atmosphere. Soil microorganisms are able to metabolize carbon monoxide to carbon dioxide. By some estimates, this process removes almost as much atmospheric carbon monoxide as anthropogenic sources produce annually.

> **The personal automobile is the single most important anthropogenic source of CO.**

Health Effects of Carbon Monoxide

Carbon monoxide begins to exert noticeable health effects at relatively low concentrations. At less than 30 ppm, it may cause impairment of central nervous system functions. A person may be able to see less clearly and may carry out normal psychomotor activities less efficiently. In the range between 30 and 60 ppm, the gas begins to produce changes in cardiac and pulmonary functions. Finally, at levels greater than 60 ppm, the effects are life-threatening, including headache, fatigue, drowsiness, coma, respiratory failure, and ultimately death.

In general, the health effects produced by carbon monoxide—and any other pollutant—depend on two factors: the concentration of the pollutant and the length of time that one is exposed to the pollutant. In the case of carbon monoxide, exposure to a concentration of about 1,000 ppm for one hour is roughly comparable to exposure to a 200-ppm concentration for five hours.

> **Carbon monoxide causes health effects because of its ability to react with hemoglobin.**

Health standards for carbon monoxide and other pollutants (such as those listed in Table 5) are usually phrased in terms of the amount of time exposed to a certain concentration of pollutant.

Carbon monoxide causes these health effects because of its ability to react with hemoglobin, the molecule that transports oxygen from the lungs to cells throughout the body. The reaction that occurs between hemoglobin and oxygen results in the formation of a relatively unstable complex, oxyhemoglobin (HbO_2):

$$Hb + O_2 \rightarrow HbO_2$$

High concentrations of oxygen in the pulmonary arteries drive this equilibrium to the right, resulting in the formation of more oxyhemoglobin molecules. In the capillaries surrounding cells, the concentration of oxygen is low. The equilibrium shifts to the left, releasing oxygen and allowing it to be transported across cell membranes into cell interiors. Note that the relatively weak bond between oxygen and hemoglobin allows this easy transfer of oxygen from the HbO_2 complex to the cells, where it is used for the production of energy.

Carbon monoxide also forms a complex with hemoglobin, carboxyhemoglobin (HbCO). The carboxyhemoglobin complex is much more stable than is oxyhemoglobin. The equilibrium constant for the reaction among CO, O_2, and their hemoglobin complexes is very large:

$$CO(g) + HbO_2(aq) \leftrightharpoons HbCO(aq) + O_2(g),$$

for which the equilibrium constant K_c is given by:

$$Kc = \frac{[HbCO][O_2]}{[CO][HbO_2]} = 210$$

Thus, the presence of carbon monoxide, even in low concentrations, can drive this reaction to the right, reducing the number of oxyhemoglobin molecules and increasing the relative number of more stable carboxyhemoglobin molecules. As a consequence, fewer and fewer oxygen molecules reach cells, and cells begin to die of oxygen starvation.

The first equation above illustrates a relatively straightforward method for dealing with carbon-monoxide poisoning. Putting a patient in an atmosphere of pure oxygen drives this reaction to the left, expelling carbon monoxide from the complex with hemoglobin, and forming more oxyhemoglobin.

Controlling Carbon-Monoxide Pollution

Carbon-monoxide pollution can be reduced if the efficiency of fossil fuel combustion systems (especially those used in motor vehicles) is increased. In general, two methods are used to achieve this goal. The first is the **catalytic converter,** whose design is shown in Figure 7. This device is sometimes known as a three-way catalytic converter because it acts on three important gases released from an internal combustion engine: carbon monoxide, oxides of nitrogen, and hydrocarbons.

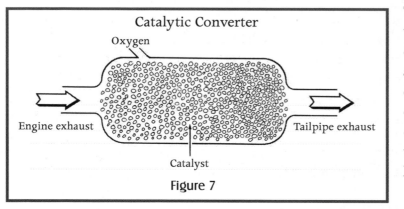

Catalytic Converter

Oxygen

Engine exhaust

Tailpipe exhaust

Catalyst

Figure 7

The catalytic converter consists of two chambers, each of which contains very small ceramic beads or a honeycomb-shaped filter containing a catalyst. In the first chamber, the catalyst (usually finely divided rhodium metal) helps reduce the unburned hydrocarbons to hydrogen gas and carbon monoxide.

$$2HC + 2H_2O \rightarrow 3H_2 + 2CO$$

The H_2 + CO produced in this reaction then reacts with oxides of nitrogen in the vehicle's exhaust gases, forming harmless nitrogen gas, carbon dioxide, and water.

$$2NO + 2H_2 \rightarrow N_2 + 2H_2O$$

$$2NO + 2CO \rightarrow N_2 + 2CO_2$$

$$2NO_2 + 4CO \rightarrow N_2 + 4CO_2$$

These gases and remaining exhaust gases then pass into the second chamber of the catalytic converter. In this chamber, the catalyst (usually consisting of a mixture of finely divided platinum and palladium) catalyzes the oxidation of carbon monoxide and any remaining hydrocarbons to carbon dioxide and water.

$$2CO + O_2 \rightarrow 2CO_2$$

$$4HC + 5O_2 \rightarrow 4CO_2 + 2H_2O$$

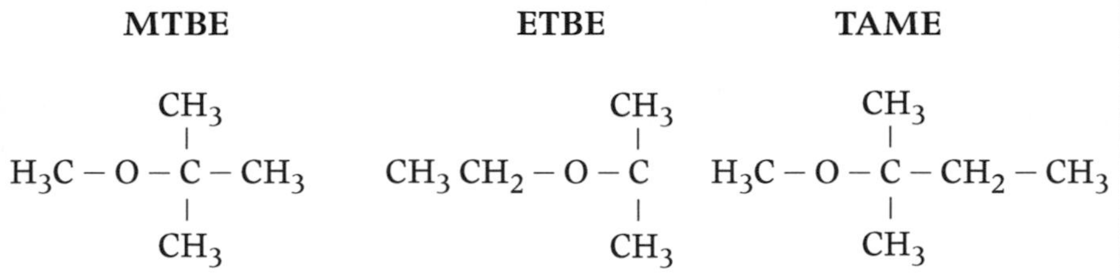

MTBE   ETBE   TAME

$$CH_3$$
$$|$$
$$H_3C - O - C - CH_3$$
$$|$$
$$CH_3$$

$$CH_3$$
$$|$$
$$CH_3CH_2 - O - C$$
$$|$$
$$CH_3$$

$$CH_3$$
$$|$$
$$H_3C - O - C - CH_2 - CH_3$$
$$|$$
$$CH_3$$

Figure 8

A second approach to the reduction of carbon-monoxide emissions has been to modify the composition of gasoline by adding certain chemicals that increase the amount of oxygen available to support combustion. Such fuels are known as *oxygenated gasoline, reformulated gasoline,* or *oxygas.* The additives used in oxygas are alcohols and ethers, most commonly ethanol (ethyl alcohol) and methyl tertiary-butyl ether (MTBE). Two less commonly used additives are ethyl tertiary-butyl ether (ETBE) and tertiary-amyl methyl ether (TAME) (Figure 8).

The use of oxygenated fuels was first mandated by the Clean Air Act amendments of 1990. This legislation required petroleum companies to sell oxygenated gas at certain times of the year and in certain areas where carbon-monoxide emissions were greatest. This program went into effect in 1995 and was expanded in 2000 to include more affected areas.

Ethanol- and MTBE-enriched gasoline have both been effective in reducing carbon-monoxide emissions. The former product, also known as *gasohol,* has been somewhat less popular than gas containing MTBE because of gasohol's higher cost. However, environmental problems associated with MTBE may ultimately force an increased reliance on gasohol in programs for reducing carbon-monoxide emissions.

The problem with MTBE is its tendency to leak from storage tanks into the ground, polluting groundwater. Since MTBE has been listed by the U.S. Environmental Protection Agency as a potential human carcinogen (cancer-causing agent), many individuals and organizations have called for an end to the use of MTBE as a fuel additive. At the early part of this century, some states revised regulations controlling the sale of oxygas that contains MTBE, and the petroleum industry began to look for alternatives for reformulated gasoline.

EXPLORE   **Exploration Activities**

1. Describe some processes by which CO is added to and removed from the atmosphere.

2. Write a chemical equation that shows how CO causes health problems in humans.

3. What is the primary technique being used to control CO pollution?

4. What is reformulated gasoline? What compounds are used in making this product?

BACKGROUND

> **Bacterial action accounts for about 90% of all nitrogen oxides in the atmosphere.**

Nitrogen Oxides

Since the first Clean Air Act was passed in 1965, the concentration of every major air pollutant has declined in the United States, with the sole exception of nitrogen oxides. Current emissions of about 24 million metric tons per year are about 10% higher than they were in 1970. The primary reason for this increase has been an increase in emissions from non-road and diesel engines.

Sources and Sinks

The largest single source of nitrogen oxides in the atmosphere is bacterial action in soil. Bacteria produce both nitrous oxide (N_2O) and nitric oxide (NO). Bacterial action accounts for about 90% of all nitrogen oxides in the atmosphere.

The major anthropogenic source of nitrogen oxides in the United States is internal combustion engines used in transportation, electric power generating plants, and factories. These sources account for about 95% of all anthropogenic nitrogen oxides released into the atmosphere, about half from motor vehicles and about 25% from each of the other two sources.

Virtually all of the nitrogen oxide in polluted air is produced by the reaction between elemental nitrogen and oxygen in the atmosphere. The reaction between these gases has a low probability at ambient temperature because of the strong bonds between nitrogen atoms and between oxygen atoms. Breaking the oxygen–oxygen bond requires 118 kilocalories/mole (kcal/mole) of energy, and breaking the nitrogen–nitrogen bond requires 225 kcal/mole. The overall reaction between the two elements is, therefore, highly endothermic.

$$N_2(g) + O_2(g) \rightarrow 2NO(g); H = 180.8 \text{ kilojoules (kJ) (at } 25°C)$$

As the temperature increases, the equilibrium in this reaction shifts to the right, and the rate at which NO forms increases rapidly. Also, the equilibrium concentration of NO increases. In a typical internal combustion engine, a concentration of 500 ppm nitric oxide is produced in 23 minutes at about 1,300°C and in 0.12 seconds at about 2,000°C.

Emission gases from an internal combustion engine contain insignificantly small concentrations of nitrogen dioxide (NO_2). That gas is produced in the reaction between NO and O_2.

$$2NO(g) + O_2(g) \rightarrow 2NO_2(g)$$

Chemists are still unsure about what conditions lead to the formation of nitrogen dioxide. The kinetics of the direct synthesis from NO and O_2 are too slow to cause the rapid buildup of NO_2 in the atmosphere. Some more complex series of reactions must result in the final production of NO_2. One possibility is the reaction of NO with ozone:

$$NO(g) + O_3(g) \rightarrow NO_2 + O_2(g)$$

Other possibilities are the reaction of NO with the hydroperoxyl radical ($HOO\cdot$) or with the methylperoxyl radical ($H_3COO\cdot$):

$$HOO\cdot + NO \rightarrow NO_2 + HO\cdot$$

$$H_3COO\cdot + NO \rightarrow NO_2 + H_3CO\cdot$$

N_2O produced by bacterial action eventually finds its way into the stratosphere. There, solar radiation provides the energy to convert N_2O into NO:

$$2N_2O \rightarrow 2NO + N_2$$

$$2N_2O \rightarrow 2N_2 + O_2$$

NO from either natural or anthropogenic sources is converted in the troposphere into NO_2, and then into nitrous and nitric acids (HNO_2 and HNO_3, respectively).

$$2NO + O_2 \rightarrow 2NO_2$$

$$2NO_2 + H_2O \rightarrow HNO_2 + HNO_3$$

The nitrogen acids are then washed from the atmosphere by rain or some other form of deposition.

> **N_2O produced by bacterial action eventually finds its way into the stratosphere.**

Environmental Effects of Nitrogen Oxides

Nitrogen oxides exert their effects on the environment in the form of oxides and acids. As described above, NO_2 in the atmosphere reacts with water to form both nitrous and nitric acids. Again, the direct reaction of NO_2 with water does not occur rapidly enough to account for the actual, observed levels of nitrogen acids in the atmosphere. Therefore, more complex reactions are involved in the conversion of the oxides into the acids. Here are some possible processes:

$$2NO_2 + O_3(g) \rightarrow N_2O_5(g) + O_2(g)$$

followed by

$$N_2O_5(g) + H_2O(l) \rightarrow 2HNO_3(aq)$$

or

$$HO\cdot + NO(g) + M \rightarrow HNO_3(aq) + M$$

where M = some active species

or

$$NO_2(g) + O(g) + M \rightarrow NO_3(g) + M$$

followed by

$$NO_2(g) + NO_3(g) \rightarrow N_2O_5(g)$$

followed by

$$N_2O_5(g) + H_2O(l) \rightarrow 2HNO_3(aq)$$

> **Nitrogen oxides damage leaves, flowers, fruits, and other plant structures.**

The effects of nitrogen oxides on inorganic and organic materials often result from the conversion of these oxides to nitric acid. Nitric acid attacks metals, marble, limestone, and other building materials. Nitrogen oxides also damage leaves, flowers, fruits, and other plant structures. At levels of only 3 ppm, nitrogen oxides have been observed to cause spotting on the leaves of pinto beans and suppressed the growth of the plant.

Nitrogen oxides also have harmful effects on animals. Nitrogen dioxide in particular irritates the mucous membranes, damages cells, and contributes to respiratory and cardiac problems. In experiments conducted at very high concentrations of nitrogen oxide, mice, rats, rabbits, and other animals have experienced respiratory problems, pulmonary edema (accumulation of fluids in the lungs), and death.

Very large doses of nitrogen oxides can have similar effects on humans. Individuals exposed to concentrations of 100 ppm for an hour or less may experience nasal irritation, breathing discomfort, respiratory distress, pulmonary edema, and even death.

One possible mechanism by which nitrogen oxides cause biological effects is the formation of nitrogen acids as the oxides dissove in intracellular and intercellular water in organisms.

So far, there is no evidence of serious acute damage resulting from the levels of nitrogen oxides found in even moderately polluted air. However, it is reasonable to expect some long-term chronic health effects among individuals who are exposed over many years to the levels of nitrogen oxides found in polluted air.

Controlling Nitrogen-Oxide Pollution

The mechanisms for controlling nitrogen-oxide emissions are different for stationary sources (such as power plants and factories) and for mobile (vehicular) sources. The three-way catalytic converter, discussed on page 42, is the method most commonly used in vehicles. The problem for stationary sources is somewhat more complicated.

Oxides of nitrogen are formed at the high temperatures at which industrial combustion reactions occur. So the simplest approach to reducing emissions is to reduce the temperatures at which the industrial processes take place. But that also reduces the efficiency and economic viability of the plants and factories.

One solution to this dilemma is the development of a two-stage combustion system. Stage one takes place at an elevated temperature that results in a highly efficient combustion reaction (and the consequent formation of NO). However, oxygen is supplied to the fuel in a concentration slightly less than what is needed to oxidize the fuel completely. The lack of excess oxygen reduces the likelihood that oxides of nitrogen will form.

> **Some substance is injected into flue gases that will reduce NO to elemental nitrogen, a harmless product.**

In the second stage of the operation, the combustion temperature is reduced, thus making nitric-oxide formation less likely. At the same time, excess oxygen gas is provided. Fuel remaining after the first stage is largely burned off in the second stage.

Another method of controlling nitrogen-oxide emissions is to remove NO from flue gases after combustion has occurred. Usually, some substance is injected into the flue gases that will reduce NO to elemental nitrogen, a harmless product. Additives used in this approach include carbon monoxide, methane, and ammonia, resulting in reactions such as the following:

$$2CO(g) + 2NO(g) \rightarrow N_2(g) + 2CO_2(g)$$

$$CH_4(g) + 4NO(g) \rightarrow 2N_2(g) + CO_2(g) + 2H_2O(l)$$

$$4NH_3(g) + 6NO(g) \rightarrow 5N_2(g) + 6H_2O(l)$$

 **Exploration Activities**

1. How does temperature affect the formation of NO and NO_2?

2. How are nitrogen oxides converted to nitrogen acids in the atmosphere?

BACKGROUND

> **The most important natural source of SO$_2$ is volcanic eruptions.**

Sulfur Dioxide

Of the two oxides of sulfur, sulfur dioxide (SO$_2$) and sulfur trioxide (SO$_3$), the former is far more abundant in the atmosphere. One reason is that the conversion of SO$_2$ to SO$_3$ occurs very slowly. Also, once formed, SO$_3$ tends to react rapidly with water droplets in the air to form sulfuric acid, H$_2$SO$_4$.

Sources and Sinks

The most important natural source of SO$_2$ is volcanic eruptions. Some of the gas from such eruptions is produced directly as SO$_2$, and some is formed during the oxidation of hydrogen sulfide (H$_2$S), also released during an eruption.

$$2H_2S(g) + 3O_2(g) \rightarrow 2SO_2(g) + 2H_2O(l)$$

Hydrogen sulfide is also produced during the decay of organic matter on Earth. When oxidized by atmospheric oxygen (and perhaps ozone), hydrogen sulfide produces SO$_2$.

$$H_2S(g) + O_3(g) \rightarrow SO_2(g) + H_2O(l)$$

Experts estimate that about 25×10^9 kg of SO$_2$ is produced and released annually by natural sources.

The most important anthropogenic source of sulfur oxides (primarily SO$_2$) is the combustion of coal and oil. The burning of coal for heat and to produce electricity is probably the largest single source of these pollutants. In coal, sulfur typically occurs in the form of iron pyrites, FeS$_2$, or in organic compounds. Burning of coal in plants converts the sulfur to SO$_2$.

$$4FeS_2 + 11O_2(g) \rightarrow 2Fe_2O_3(s) + 8SO_2(g)$$

$$S \text{ (in organic compounds)} + O_2(g) \rightarrow SO_2(g)$$

Petroleum refining and smelting of ores constitute another important anthropogenic source of sulfur dioxide.

$$2ZnS(s) + 3O_2(g) \rightarrow 2ZnO(s) + 2SO_2(g)$$

> ## Once in the atmosphere, SO₂ is oxidized to SO₃.

All of the above reactions result primarily in the formation of the quadrivalent (+4) oxide, SO_2. Very little hexavalent (+6) oxide, SO_3, is produced directly. In addition, only small quantities of SO_2 are converted to SO_3, since the equilibrium in the following reaction lies far to the left at almost all temperatures:

$$2SO_2(g) + O_2(g) \rightleftarrows 2SO_3(g)$$

Once in the atmosphere, however, SO_2 is oxidized to SO_3. The process apparently does not involve a simple, direct combination of compound and element, as shown in the above equation. As noted above, the thermodynamics of the reaction are unfavorable for the formation of SO_3 at almost all temperatures. Instead, the reaction involves other species, including H_2O_2, O_3, $HO\cdot$, water and salts of manganese and iron, as well as the SO_2 and O_2 reactants themselves. The specific reaction that occurs depends on the types and concentrations of species present and on the moisture content of the air. Some of the proposed mechanisms for the conversion of SO_2 to SO_3 include:

$$SO_2 + O_3 \rightarrow SO_3 + O_2$$

and

$$SO_2 + HO\cdot \rightarrow HSO_3\cdot$$

followed by

$$HSO_3\cdot + O_2 \rightarrow HSO_5\cdot$$

followed by

$$HSO_5\cdot + NO \rightarrow HSO_4\cdot + NO_2$$

followed by

$$HSO_4\cdot + NO_2 + H_2O \rightarrow H_2SO_4 + HNO_3$$

and

$$2SO_2 + 2H_2O + O_2 \xrightarrow{\text{Fe and Mn salts}} 2H_2SO_4$$

In the last mechanism shown above, sulfur dioxide and oxygen both dissolve in droplets of sulfuric acid. The presence of manganese and iron salts as catalysts then makes possible the conversion of SO_2 to SO_3 (in the form of H_2SO_4).

The catalysts needed for the conversion of SO_2 to SO_3 in this reaction, salts of iron and manganese, are generally available in the atmosphere. Both occur as trace elements in coal. They are commonly released, along with SO_2, in flue gases of power plants, chemical factories, and other industrial and heating operations.

Sulfur in the atmosphere is eventually converted to its hexavalent (+6) form as SO_3 or SO_4^{2-}. In either case, it ultimately appears in the form of sulfuric acid, H_2SO_4, or less commonly as some metallic sulfate.

Acids and sulfates are removed from the atmosphere by rain, snow, or some other form of precipitation, or by settling out as a dry deposit on the earth's surface. Notice also that the mechanism represented by the equations suggests that nitric acid may be formed along with sulfuric acid during the oxidation of SO_2.

Environmental Effects of Sulfur Oxides

Sulfur dioxide and sulfuric acid cause damage to buildings, plants, and animals. Marble, limestone, and other building materials are destroyed by sulfuric acid. Marble and limestone are forms of calcium carbonate, $CaCO_3$. The reaction that occurs between the stone and acid is:

$$CaCO_3(s) + H_2SO_4(aq) \rightarrow CaSO_4(aq) + H_2O + CO_2(g)$$

The solubility of $CaSO_4$, 9.1×10^{-6}, is about 100 times greater than that of $CaCO_3$, 2.8×10^{-9}. The sulfate, therefore, is considerably more likely to dissolve than the carbonate. As a result, stone buildings, bridges, statues, and other structures are dissolved by this process over long periods of time.

Sulfur dioxide and the sulfuric acid it produces in the atmosphere also damage plants. The damage includes spotting on leaves, decreased growth, loss of leaves, low yield of fruit, and the death of the plant. On the other hand, sulfur is also an essential micronutrient for plants and animals. A **micronutrient** is an element needed in very small amounts in order to maintain the health of an organism. Under some circumstances, the addition of small amounts of sulfur may actually be beneficial, especially to certain types of plants.

> **Sulfur dioxide and sulfuric acid cause damage to buildings, plants, and animals.**

> ## Sulfur dioxide poses especially serious problems for individuals already suffering from respiratory problems.

The effects of sulfur dioxide on human health depend on the concentration of the pollutant and the length of exposure. Humans can recognize the characteristic odor of sulfur dioxide at concentrations as low as 0.5 ppm. At concentrations of 1.5 ppm, the gas begins to produce constriction of the bronchi, with some impairment of breathing. At higher concentrations, a normal, healthy person will experience throat and eye irritation (about 100 ppm) and eventually, severe coughing and choking reactions (200 ppm). Sulfur dioxide poses especially serious problems for individuals already suffering from respiratory problems, such as emphysema and chronic bronchitis.

Controlling Sulfur-Dioxide Pollution

There are two widely used methods for reducing SO_2 emissions. The first involves the removal of sulfur from coal before it is burned. The second involves the removal of SO_2 from flue gases after combustion.

The most desirable approach is to use coal and oil with low concentrations of sulfur. The combustion of coal with less than 0.7% sulfur produces levels of SO_2 that fall within acceptable EPA limits (Table 2.6). This option becomes less realistic, however, as the world's coal reserves decrease. Over time, it will become prohibitively expensive to use only the highest-quality fuels—that is, coal and oil with very low sulfur content.

Chemists have tried, therefore, to develop other techniques for removing sulfur from coal before combustion. One method involves the conversion of solid coal to a gaseous fuel in the process known as **gasification.** In this process, sulfur is converted to gaseous hydrogen sulfide, H_2S, which can then be separated from the gaseous fuel by standard chemical procedures.

The second method for removing sulfur from coal is by liquefaction. In this process, coal and hydrogen are reacted together at temperatures of 400°C to 450°C and pressures of 100 to 300 atm. The major product of this reaction is a heavy, petroleum-like liquid that can be treated like coal oil. Sulfur is converted to H_2S, which can then be removed from the liquefied coal product.

Today the most common technique for the control of SO_2 is to remove the gas from smokestacks after combustion, generally making use of some kind of reaction between SO_2 and a basic solution. An example is the lime-slurry scrubbing process, in which calcium hydroxide ($Ca(OH)_2$) is the basic substance used.

$$SO_2(g) + Ca(OH)_2(aq) \rightarrow CaSO_3(aq) + H_2O$$

Acid Deposition

Recall that atmospheric reactions involving SO_2 and nitrogen oxides ultimately result in the formation of sulfuric and nitric acids. In addition, carbon dioxide in the atmosphere dissolves in water droplets to produce an acidic solution:

$$CO_2(g) + H_2O \rightleftharpoons H^+(aq) + HCO_3^-(aq)$$

These acids are carried to Earth's surface in a variety of ways. **Dry deposition** occurs when acid molecules adsorb to very small solid particles in the atmosphere. When these particles fall to the earth, they carry the adsorbed acids with them. Scientists believe that dry deposition accounts for the removal of no more than 20% of all acid molecules formed in the atmosphere.

A second method by which acids are removed from the atmosphere is **wet deposition.** The term refers to rain, snow, and other forms of precipitation that contain acidic molecules. The major atmospheric acids are all soluble in water. They tend to dissolve in water droplets within or outside of clouds. When these droplets coalesce to form larger water droplets or snowflakes and fall to the earth, they carry the dissolved acids with them. One of the most common instances of this is called **acid rain.**

> **The major atmospheric acids are all soluble in water.**

As a consequence of these reactions, various forms of precipitation are normally acidic, with a pH of about 5 to 6. Fog banks also reflect this pattern, having pH values similar to those for rain, snow, hail, and other forms of wet deposition.

In recent decades, precipitation with pH values much lower than those of normal precipitation have been measured in several locations. Some parts of Canada and the northeastern United States, for example, have reported rainfall with a pH of 4.0 or less. Similar readings have been made in western Europe and Scandinavia. The most acidic rain ever measured, at Hubbard Brook, New Hampshire, had a pH of 2.2, about equal to that of lemon juice or stomach acid.

The areas where the most acidic deposition has been measured lie to the east of three major power-generating areas: the midwestern United States, the Midlands of Great Britain, and the Ruhr Valley along the French-German border. Many scientists now believe that acid deposition is the result of the combustion of fossil fuels in these industrialized areas.

The scenario by which acid deposition is produced may be as follows: Sulfur and nitrogen oxides are released during the combustion of fossil fuels. Very tall smokestacks carry these gases hundreds of meters into the air. Prevailing winds carry the gases from west to east. Some studies show the gases may travel more than 4,000 km in less than a week.

As they pass through the atmosphere, oxides of sulfur and nitrogen react with water droplets to form sulfuric and nitric acids. These tiny droplets of acid eventually coalesce into drops large enough to fall to Earth as rain, snow, hail, or some other form of precipitation. They may also hover above the ground as a low cloud or fog.

Ironically, pollution control devices at the site of combustion may actually contribute to the problem of acid deposition. In the first place, very tall smokestacks have been constructed on many plants in order to reduce the amount of *local* pollution produced by fossil fuel combustion. These smokestacks have reduced the amount of pollution released in the immediate area of the plant. However, they have assured that pollutant gases spread out over a much wider region, especially to the east of the plants.

Also, pollution control devices often remove fly ash from effluent gases. Compounds in fly ash tend to be basic. Thus, effluent gases with fly ash tend to contain basic compounds that will react with acids formed from oxides of sulfur and nitrogen. Removal of the fly ash by pollution control devices, then, may eliminate some of the compounds that would otherwise help to neutralize nitric and sulfuric acids in the atmosphere.

Effects of Acid Deposition

Many authorities believe that acid deposition poses a threat to inorganic materials, aquatic organisms, trees, crops, and other plants and animals. Some of the earliest effects of acid rain were

> **Ironically, pollution control devices at the site of combustion may actually contribute to the problem of acid deposition.**

56

observed in forests that had been exposed to acid deposition. More than half the trees in the Black Forest of Germany, for example, experienced leaf damage, premature loss of leaves, or reduced growth. Many trees have been killed outright. Similar effects have been observed in Scandinavia, eastern Canada, and the northeastern United States.

Research has shown that this damage can occur in a number of ways. Acid deposition damages stomata on leaves and destroys root hair. It also leaches minerals from the soil. As a result of these changes, a plant's ability to gather and use nutrients and water may be inhibited.

Acid deposition may also cause the death of aquatic organisms. Studies show that lake trout die at a pH of less than 5.0, smallmouth bass at a pH below 6.0, and mussels at a pH of less than 6.5. Fish eggs and young fry seem to be especially susceptible to acidic solutions. Even when mature fish do survive, their offspring often do not, and certain species simply die out in acidified lakes.

One mechanism by which acid deposition kills organisms is through the leaching of toxic minerals from the soil. Ions that are potentially toxic to organisms are naturally present in the soil. But these ions are commonly present in the form of compounds that are insoluble in natural groundwater of a pH greater than about 6. The addition of atmospheric acids reduces the pH of groundwater and converts these insoluble compounds to soluble forms.

One example is aluminum. Acid deposition may free Al^{3+} ions from insoluble $Al(OH)_3$ normally present in the soil, as shown in the following equation:

$$Al(OH)_3(s) + 3H^+(aq) \rightarrow Al^{3+}(aq) + 3H_2O$$

The soluble Al^{3+} ions may then be taken up by plant roots or ingested by animals, exerting their toxic effects.

Damage to lakes, rivers, and streams exposed to acid deposition has long been a matter of concern to experts. As the pH of a body of water drops, so does its ability to sustain aquatic life. In some cases, the water may become so acidic that it can no longer support any kind of plant or animal life, and the lake is said to be dead. By some estimates, more than 20% of the lakes in the Adirondack

> **Certain species of fish simply die out in acidified lakes.**

Mountains of the eastern United States fit this description. They are essentially barren of any kind of life.

The ability of lakes and rivers to respond to acidification depends largely on their location. If the riverbed or lake bottom consists of basic materials, such as hydroxides or carbonates, neutralization reactions will correct the effects of the acid deposition. For example, in lakes or rivers with limestone bottoms, acid deposition is neutralized by the following reaction:

$$2H^+(aq) + CaCO_3(s) \rightarrow Ca^{2+}(aq) + H_2O + CO_2(g)$$

If the lake or river bottom contains sandstone, however, no such neutralization can occur because sandstone (primarily SiO_2) does not react with acids. Acid from acidic rain or snow, therefore, continues to collect in the river or lake until its pH reaches dangerously low levels.

> **If the riverbed or lake bottom consists of basic materials, neutralization reactions will correct the effects of the acid deposition.**

Controlling Acid Deposition

How serious are the environmental effects of acid deposition? That question has been debated vigorously by scientific researchers, politicians, and government officials for many years. Probably the most important government effort to answer the question was initiated in 1980 when President Jimmy Carter authorized the creation of the National Acid Precipitation Program (NAPAP). Conclusions of the NAPAP study on acid deposition were reported in 1990. In general, they suggested that damage from acid deposition was much less serious than scientists had thought. Some conclusions of the study were:

1. "There are no measurable and consistent effects [from acid deposition] on crop yield." In fact, acid deposition may actually "benefit crops indirectly through the nutritional enrichment of agricultural soils."

2. "The vast majority of forests in the United States and Canada are not affected by [acid deposition]."

3. "Only 4.2% of a sample of lakes [in the United States] had lost all ability to neutralize acid inputs."

The NAPAP conclusions were not well-received by many scientists and government officials in the United States and Canada. NAPAP researchers were criticized for choosing data selectively and interpreting it incorrectly. But that debate turned out to be moot. Just as the NAPAP conclusions were being reported, the U.S. Congress was adopting the Clean Air Act Amendments of 1990. One of the provisions of this act was the establishment of a Clean Air Program within the EPA. The mission of the new agency was to develop methods for reducing sulfur and nitrogen-oxide emissions and thereby reducing the level of acid deposition in the United States and Canada.

Ten years after the Acid Rain Program was created, the agency was able to say that it had good news and bad news. The good news was that sulfur dioxide emissions in the United States had been reduced by about 17% between 1990 and 2000. The bad news was that emissions of nitrogen oxides had increased by about 2%. Overall, studies seemed to suggest that any improvements in the quality of lakes and streams, forests, and other parts of the environment were modest, at best.

In late 1999, Sen. Patrick Leahy (D-Vt.) and Rep. John Sweeney (R-N.Y.) asked the General Accounting Office to study the acid deposition program and assess its accomplishments. The GAO confirmed the EPA's reports of decreased SO_2 and steady nitrogen oxide emissions. It also confirmed significant decreases in sulfate concentrations in eastern lakes, but found significant increases in nitrate concentrations. It was not clear why lakes and rivers would continue to be gaining acidity from nitrates when nitrogen oxide emissions were holding steady. One of the troubling conclusions of the GAO study was the agency's concerns that some bodies of water in the eastern United States might have been so badly damaged that they may never recover at all. (You can read the GAO report at www.gao.gov/ on the Internet.)

> **Studies seemed to suggest that any improvements in the environment were modest, at best.**

EXPLORE   **Exploration Activities**

1. Write a series of chemical equations that describe how sulfur dioxide is produced by human activities and then converted into acids in the atmosphere.

2. How is sulfur dioxide removed from flue gases?

3. Explain how soil composition can modify the effects of acid deposition.

4. List some effects of acid rain on the environment.

BACKGROUND

> **Hydrocarbons are a source of concern not only because of the hazards they pose, but also because some of them are precursors to photochemical oxidants.**

Hydrocarbons

Two important classes of air pollutants produced during the incomplete combustion of fossil fuels are hydrocarbons and particulates. Hydrocarbons are a source of concern not only because of the hazards they pose, but also because some of them are precursors to photochemical oxidants, which are sometimes even more toxic than hydrocarbons themselves. The particulates constitute a large class of pollutants produced during combustion and as the result of many mining and manufacturing operations.

Hydrocarbons are compounds that contain only hydrogen and carbon. Tens of thousands of such compounds exist. To make the study of hydrocarbons simpler, chemists subdivide these compounds into several families. The hydrocarbon families are determined by their molecular structures.

One way of distinguishing hydrocarbons is whether the carbon atoms in the molecule are joined in a closed ring, as shown in the formula for benzene in Figure 9 (next page), or in an open chain, as shown in the formula for propane. Hydrocarbons that have a structure similar to that of benzene are called **aromatic hydrocarbons.** Those whose molecules consist of open chains are called **aliphatic hydrocarbons.**

Hydrocarbons may be further distinguished by the type of bonding between carbon atoms. If only carbon–carbon single bonds are present, the hydrocarbon is called an **alkane.** Alkanes are also known as **saturated hydrocarbons.** If one or more carbon–carbon double bonds exist, the compound is an **alkene.** The term **unsaturated hydrocarbon** is also used for alkenes.

Still other hydrocarbon molecules are different and often more complex than the families described above. The **terpene** molecule, alpha-terpene, shown in Figure 9, is an example of such a molecule.

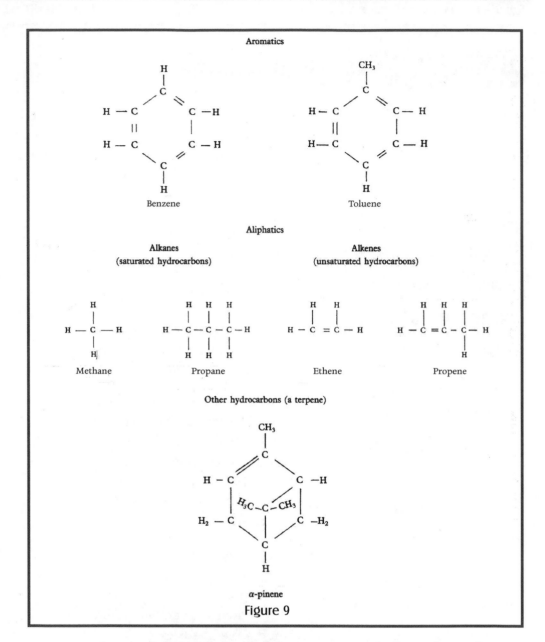

Figure 9

The symbol HC is often used to represent a hydrocarbon. The general formula RH is also used to represent members of this family. In this formula, *R* stands for an alkyl or aryl group, an aliphatic or aromatic hydrocarbon with one hydrogen atom missing.

Hydrocarbons are members of a larger group of environmentally important compounds called **volatile organic compounds** (VOCs). VOCs are carbon-containing compounds that exist as gases or that vaporize easily. Some of the most common VOCs found in polluted air are the hydrocarbons benzene, toluene, xylene, ethylbenzene, hexane, 1,3-butadiene, and polyaromatic hydrocarbons (PAHs), as well as formaldehyde, butanal, hexanal, acetone, and ethanol.

Sources and Sinks

Some hydrocarbons exist in unpolluted air. Methane, the most common hydrocarbon, is produced by the decay of organic matter by anaerobic bacteria. According to some authorities, the digestion of cellulose by termites may be the largest single source of methane in the world. Methane constitutes the seventh most abundant gas in the atmosphere with an average worldwide concentration of about 1.4 ppm.

Only about 15% of all hydrocarbons in the atmosphere come from anthropogenic sources. Slightly more than half of these sources are associated with the transportation industry. Hydrocarbons are released into the atmosphere at nearly every stage in the use of motor vehicles: during fueling, as the result of the incomplete combustion of fuel, and by evaporation from engines. Other major anthropogenic sources of hydrocarbons include petroleum refineries, evaporation of organic solvents, agricultural burning, solid-waste disposal, and industrial chemical processes.

The fate of hydrocarbons in the atmosphere is a complex question. Different categories of hydrocarbons undergo quite different reactions. Some hydrocarbons are relatively stable. They normally do not react with most chemical species present in the atmosphere. Alkanes, especially those with branching side chains, are typical of these relatively inactive hydrocarbons.

On the other hand, alkenes and aromatics are relatively susceptible to oxidation in the atmosphere. The products of the atmospheric degradation of these hydrocarbons include CO_2 and H_2O, as well as many complex organic compounds. The next section describes some of the most environmentally interesting of those reactions.

Photochemical Oxidants

Some hydrocarbons exert harmful effects on the environment by themselves. For example, benzene (C_6H_6) is known to be carcinogenic. A carcinogen is a chemical known to cause cancer in humans and/or other animals. Often, a more serious hazard posed by the hydrocarbons results from other compounds formed in

> **The fate of hydrocarbons in the atmosphere is a complex question.**

chemical reactions that the hydrocarbons undergo in the atmosphere. Those other compounds are the **photochemical oxidants,** oxidizing agents produced by light-catalyzed reactions.

One of the most abundant photochemical oxidants is ozone, which is not a hydrocarbon. Ozone production begins when sunlight acting on an oxygen molecule causes the molecule's dissociation into two atoms of oxygen.

$$O_2 \xrightarrow{\quad h\upsilon \quad} 2O$$

where $h\upsilon$ represents a photon, the basic unit of electromagnetic energy, including light.

The role of light in bringing about this reaction accounts for the name *photochemical* reaction.

Atomic oxygen (O) is highly reactive and may combine with a second molecule of oxygen to form ozone.

$$O + O_2 + M \rightarrow O_3 + M$$

where M represents some third species.

The third species undergoes no chemical change in the reaction but does carry away some of the energy produced in the reaction. Without the removal of this energy, the ozone molecule would be highly energetic and would decay quickly to molecular and atomic oxygen.

$$O_3 \rightarrow O + O_2$$

Ozone is an important photochemical oxidant not only because of its own reactivity, but also because of its role in other photochemical reactions.

Among the most common of these reactions are those that involve the photochemical oxidants known as the peroxyacylnitrates. The basic structure of the peroxyacylnitrates is shown in Figure 10.

$$R - C = O \qquad \text{where } R = \text{any hydrocarbon group}$$
$$|$$
$$O - O - NO_2$$

Figure 10

One of the best-known peroxyacylnitrates is peroxyacetylnitrate (PAN), in which R in the formula of Figure 10 represents the methyl group, CH_3. Other common peroxyacylnitrates are peroxypropionylnitrate (PPN) and peroxybenzoylnitrate (PBN), shown in Figure 11.

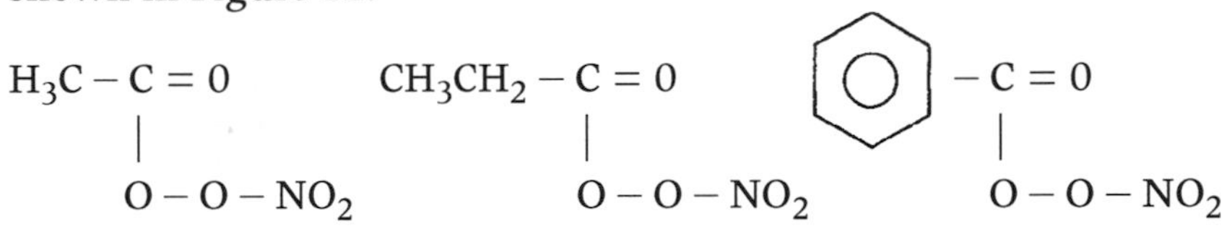

$$H_3C - C = O \qquad CH_3CH_2 - C = O \qquad \bigcirc - C = O$$
$$\qquad |\qquad\qquad\qquad\qquad |\qquad\qquad\qquad\qquad\qquad |$$
$$O - O - NO_2 \qquad\quad O - O - NO_2 \qquad\quad O - O - NO_2$$
$$\quad\text{PAN}\qquad\qquad\qquad\quad\text{PPN}\qquad\qquad\qquad\quad\text{PBN}$$

Figure 11

> **The mechanisms by which photochemical oxidants are formed is not completely understood.**

The mechanisms by which photochemical oxidants are formed is not completely understood. Chemists believe the series of reactions outlined below probably plays a major role in this process. In the first step of this series, energy from sunlight causes the dissocation of NO_2 to NO and atomic oxygen.

$$NO_2(g) \xrightarrow{\text{h}\nu} NO(g) + O(g)$$

Light plays a critical role in this reaction, explaining why it is called a **photolytic** (*photo* means *light* and *-lytic* means *breaking*) **reaction.** Next, the oxygen formed during photolysis reacts with molecular oxygen to form ozone.

$$O + O_2 \rightarrow O_3$$

In the absence of hydrocarbons, ozone reacts with NO to regenerate NO_2 and O_2, resulting in a closed cycle for the species involved.

$$O_3(g) + NO(g) \rightarrow NO_2(g) + O_2(g)$$

If hydrocarbons are present, however, they compete with NO. An example of the series of reactions that can occur between hydrocarbons and ozone is shown below. Reactions like these result in the formation of intermediary organic compounds, such as aldehydes, free radicals, and eventually a peroxyacylnitrate, in this example, PAN.

$$CH_3CH{=}CH_2 + O_3 \rightarrow CH_3{-}C{=}O + HCO\cdot + HO\cdot$$
$$\qquad\qquad\qquad\qquad\qquad\qquad |$$
$$\qquad\qquad\qquad\qquad\qquad\qquad H$$

     Propene   Ethanal   Free radicals
                       (an aldehyde)

$$\text{CH}_3\text{--C=O} + \text{O} \xrightarrow{h\upsilon} \text{CH}_3\text{--}\overset{\cdot}{\text{C}}\text{=O} + \text{OH}\cdot$$
$$\overset{|}{\text{H}}$$

$$\text{CH}_3\text{--}\overset{\cdot}{\text{C}}\text{=O} + \text{O}_2 \longrightarrow \text{CH}_3\text{--C=O}$$
$$\underset{\text{O} - \text{O}\cdot}{|}$$

$$\text{CH}_3\text{--C=O} + \text{NO}_2 \longrightarrow \text{CH}_3\text{--C=O}$$
$$\underset{\text{O} - \text{O}\cdot}{|} \qquad \underset{\underset{\text{PAN}}{\text{O} - \text{O} - \text{NO}_2}}{|}$$

> **The more widespread form of smog common in Los Angeles is chemically different from industrial smog.**

The reactions that occur in any urban atmosphere are much more complex than the simple model suggested here. Those reactions result in a condition known as smog. The term *smog* was first used in connection with the irritating atmospheric conditions in London that result from a combination of smoke and fog. More accurately, this form of air pollution is known as **industrial smog.**

The much more widespread form of smog that became common in Los Angeles and other large cities in the 1950s is chemically different from industrial smog. It results, as shown above, from the interaction of light energy and motor-vehicle emissions (NO and hydrocarbons) and is more accurately called photochemical smog.

Environmental Effects of Hydrocarbons

Hydrocarbons seem to have few harmful effects on plants. However, some hydrocarbons do have harmful effects on the health of animals, including humans. The vapors of many aromatics and alkenes, for example, may irritate the mucous membranes. In concentrations of more than 25 ppm for extended periods of time, these hydrocarbons may cause more serious damage like the formation of tumors.

Most health effects resulting from photochemical smog are the result of oxidants, such as ozone and peroxyacylnitrates, especially PAN. These compounds attack enzymes in organisms, interrupting essential biochemical functions. For example, ozone may destroy enzymes in the citric acid cycle, reducing or eliminating an organism's ability to produce the energy it needs to survive.

Visible effects of ozone and PAN on plants involve spotting and discoloration of leaves, destruction of flowers, reduction in fruit production and formation of seeds, and the death of a plant.

The most obvious effects of photochemical oxidants on human health involve the eyes and respiratory system. Red, itchy, runny eyes and an irritated throat are early symptoms of exposure to such compounds. These conditions are particularly serious for individuals who already suffer from cardiac or respiratory conditions, such as asthma, emphysema, or chronic bronchitis. Long-term exposure to photochemical oxidants increases the risk for lung and heart diseases.

> **Long-term exposure to photochemical oxidants increases the risk for lung and heart diseases.**

Control of Hydrocarbons and Photochemical Oxidants

The control of hydrocarbons and photochemical oxidants primarily involves mechanisms that have already been discussed. The use of catalytic converters in motor vehicles, for example, reduces the amount of hydrocarbons released to the air and, thus, the amount of photochemicals that may be generated from them.

Other techniques are available for reducing hydrocarbon pollutants and thereby the secondary pollutants arising from them. For example, protective shields on gasoline pumps are required in a number of states. These shields reduce the amount of fuel that escapes during the pumping of gasoline.

⊘ **EXPLORE** **Exploration Activities**

1. Write chemical formulas for an aliphatic hydrocarbon, an aromatic hydrocarbon, a saturated hydrocarbon, and an unsaturated hydrocarbon.

2. Define a photochemical oxidant.

3. Write two equations that show how ozone is produced from NO_2 emissions.

4. Name two types of smog and tell how they are different from each other.

5. Name a chemical mechanism by which photochemical oxidants damage living organisms.

6. Describe two methods by which the emission of hydrocarbons can be controlled.

BACKGROUND

Particulates

SOME TYPICAL PARTICULATE SIZES	
Particulate	**Size range, radius, in μm**
bacteria	1–15
natural fog droplets	1–40
fly ash	3–80
cement dust	10–150
coal dust	10–400
pollen	20–60
ground limestone	30–800
fertilizer dust	30–800
foundry sand	200–2,000
raindrops	500–5,000

Table 8

The term *particulate* refers to any liquid or solid particle suspended in air. Most particulates are less than 100 μm (micrometers) in diameter. Particles larger than this tend to settle out of the atmosphere rapidly. A variety of terms is used to describe particles of different sizes. Table 8 lists the sizes of some typical particulates.

Sources and Sinks

Particulates are naturally ubiquitous in the air. As winds blow across the ground, they pick up tiny particles of earth and carry them into the atmosphere. Depending on their size, these particles may remain suspended in the air for weeks, months, or even years. Other natural sources of particulates include volcanic emissions, sea spray, and plant emissions.

On a strictly quantitative basis, anthropogenic contributions to particulates in the atmosphere are small. They probably make up only about 10% of all such particles. As with other pollutants, however, the toxicity and local concentrations of anthropogenic pollutants can make them a serious problem.

For example, agriculture is an important anthropogenic source of particulates. The same winds that pick up dust particles on cultivated land may carry away particles of pesticides, herbicides, and fertilizer as well. Humans and other animals may breathe in these potentially hazardous particles.

The main anthropogenic source of particulates is a variety of industrial operations, such as stone and rock crushing; iron and steel production; transportation and storage of grain; manufacture of cement, lime, pulp, and paper; and metallurgical operations.

Fuel combustion at power plants and factories is the second most important anthropogenic source of particulates. The release of fly ash and smoke accounts for the particulates from these sources. Forest and agricultural fires are the third most important source of anthropogenic particulates.

Particles in the atmosphere normally settle out over a period of time. As they collide with one another, they may stick together and grow larger. Eventually they become too heavy to remain in suspension, and they settle to the earth.

Particles may also be washed out of the atmosphere by rain, snow, and other forms of precipitation. They may also be carried back to the earth by winds, air currents, and downdrafts.

Health Effects of Particulates

Particulates pose a number of hazards. When they accumulate in the atmosphere, they may reduce visibility, which is an aesthetic disadvantage as well as a potential hazard.

A more important health effect of particulates is their tendency to accumulate in the respiratory system, where they block intercellular spaces. The fate of particles in the respiratory system is largely determined by their size. Particles larger than about 5.0 μm are filtered out by nasal hairs or trapped in mucous membranes. Particles between about 0.5 and 5.0 μm are able to elude these defense mechanisms and work their way into the lungs. There they are deposited within the bronchioles, the tiny tubes branching off the bronchi. Within a short time, cilia that line the bronchioles normally remove these particles and sweep them into the pharynx. From there, they are swallowed or coughed up.

Particles smaller than 0.5 μm in diameter may reach the smallest structures in the lungs, the alveoli. The alveoli are tiny air sacs that line the interior of the lungs. The removal of particles from the alveoli is more difficult and takes much longer than elsewhere in the respiratory system. The time that particles remain in the alveoli may range from a few weeks to many years. While deposited in the respiratory system, these particles may cause a number of diseases.

> **A health effect of particulates is their tendency to accumulate in the respiratory system, where they block intercellular spaces.**

> **When particles block the alveoli, they reduce the lungs' ability to exchange gases.**

Inhaled particles can damage health in a variety of ways. Some—such as particles of lead, cadmium, and mercury—are toxic themselves. As they are absorbed by the blood, they begin to poison the body. Other particles may carry toxic substances adsorbed to their surfaces. The inhaled particles thus become carriers by which hazardous substances are transported into the body. Still other kinds of particles exert a purely physical effect. When they block the alveoli, they reduce the lungs' ability to exchange gases.

Control of Particulates

There are several methods for removing particulates from exhaust systems. One of the simplest uses gravity. If air remains motionless for a period of time, the particles in suspension will settle out. The heavier particles settle out more rapidly in such a system.

Gravitational effects can be increased by using a centrifuge. As waste gases spin in a centrifuge, heavier particles are thrown outward, where they can be collected and removed.

In wet collectors, effluent gases are passed through a moist atmosphere. Liquid droplets in the collector adsorb and remove certain particulate pollutants.

Finally, electrostatic precipitators can be used to remove particulate droplets. The precipitators carry electrical charges opposite those the particulate particles carry naturally or that have been added to the droplets mechanically. The force of attraction between particulates and precipitator pulls the particles out of the waste gas to a collecting surface, from which they can be removed.

Exploration Activities

1. Name three examples of natural particulates and three anthropogenic examples.

2. Explain three ways in which particulates can cause health problems.

3. How does a centrifuge remove particulates from a sample of air?

4. What physical principle is used in the design of an electrostatic precipitator?

BACKGROUND

Ozone

> **Earth's atmosphere is thought to be very different today than it was at its origin.**

In the 1960s and 1970s, humans began to worry about the huge amounts of pollutants that were being dumped into the atmosphere. Beginning in the 1980s, a new concern emerged. Humans began to realize that anthropogenic activities are making fundamental changes in the natural composition of the atmosphere. It is no longer just a matter of making the atmosphere dirty, but of changing its basic character and composition. These concerns have focused on two problems, destruction of the earth's ozone layer and global warming, popularly known as the "greenhouse effect."

Earth's atmosphere is thought to be very different today than it was at its origin. The primitive atmosphere probably consisted primarily of methane, ammonia, hydrogen, and water, with very little oxygen.

Thus, the kind of oxidation reactions that are common on Earth today—respiration, decay, and combustion, for example—were rare or absent in the primitive atmosphere. The more abundant gases present in the atmosphere were reducing agents. Recall that hydrogen atoms, for example, typically lose electrons in a chemical reaction, making them reducing agents.

Gases in the primitive atmosphere were subjected to intense ultraviolet (UV) radiation from the Sun, making possible a number of chemical reactions involving these primitive species. Thus, over millions of years, Earth's atmosphere underwent fundamental changes.

Early life evolved the process of **photosynthesis,** the conversion of carbon dioxide to organic matter, with the release of oxygen gas. Gradually, oxygen began to accumulate in the troposphere until the atmosphere took on its modern-day composition.

The accumulation of oxygen in Earth's primitive atmosphere might be thought of as the planet's first great air pollution problem. Of course, to humans today, atmospheric oxygen is anything but a problem. But consider the fact that growing concentrations of oxygen changed the earth's original atmosphere fundamentally and drastically, from a reducing atmosphere to an oxidizing atmosphere. In that respect, the buildup of oxygen could be thought of as pollution.

The appearance of oxygen in the atmosphere made possible a second important change, the formation of ozone. The reaction is similar to one that takes place during the formation of photochemical smog (page 66). At wavelengths of about 242 nm (nanometers), ultraviolet radiation brings about the dissociation of oxygen molecules into highly energetic oxygen atoms.

$$O_2 \xrightarrow{\quad \lambda \doteq 242 \text{ nm} \quad} 2O$$

One of these oxygen atoms then has the potential to react with a second oxygen molecule to form triatomic oxygen, or ozone.

$$O + O_2 + M \rightarrow O_3 + M$$

Ozone is a highly unstable molecule that will decompose readily into an oxygen atom and an oxygen molecule unless the excess energy released in the reaction shown in the above equation is carried away by some second body (M in this equation). In such a case, ozone becomes more stable.

Over the millennia, concentrations of ozone increased until they reached a maximum level of about 200 ppb (parts per billion) in the lower stratosphere. This concentration of ozone represents the point at which the rate of produced ozone from molecular and atomic oxygen balances the rate at which ozone breaks down into these components.

This layer of ozone is critical to life on Earth, because it screens out more than 99% of the ultraviolet radiation that reaches our atmosphere from the Sun. Ultraviolet radiation causes damage in nearly all forms of life. It affects two critical classes of compounds, proteins and nucleic acids. Its effect on proteins is to cause denaturation, the loss of three-dimensional structure. When proteins lose their structure, they are unable to perform their normal functions, such as catalyzing certain critical biochemical reactions in the body. The rapid destruction of proteins in bacteria and other microorganisms often results in their death. For that reason, ultraviolet light is often used as a disinfectant.

Ultraviolet radiation also destroys bonds in DNA molecules. Destruction of these bonds, in turn, makes it impossible for DNA

> **This layer of ozone screens out more than 99% of the ultraviolet radiation that reaches our atmosphere from the Sun.**

molecules to direct the production of new proteins properly. This transformation often leads to the development of cancer in animals and to deformed leaves and other structures in plants.

In humans, the most common health problem associated with exposure to ultraviolet radiation is skin cancer. Exposure to UV radiation may result in the development of the easily treatable basal-cell skin cancer, the more serious squamous-cell skin cancer, and the highly dangerous malignant melanoma.

Thus, the ozone layer provides a critical shield for earthbound organisms. The ultraviolet radiation absorbed in the ozone layer converts ozone molecules back to molecular and atomic oxygen, as shown here:

$$O_3 \xrightarrow{\quad \lambda \doteq 200 - 320 \text{ nm} \quad} O + O_2$$

followed by

$$O + O_3 \rightarrow 2O_2$$

Under normal circumstances, the rate of formation and destruction of ozone in the stratosphere is approximately constant.

Anthropogenic Effects on the Ozone Layer

Human activities have the potential for disturbing the chemical composition of the stratosphere, where the ozone layer is located, just as they do the troposphere. At least two groups of anthropogenically generated compounds pose a potential threat to the stability of the ozone layer: the oxides of nitrogen and the halogenated hydrocarbons, especially the chlorofluorocarbons.

Nitric oxide (NO) poses the most serious threat to the ozone layer of all nitrogen oxides. It reacts with ozone to produce NO_2 and O_2.

$$NO + O_3 \rightarrow NO_2 + O_2$$

The NO_2 produced in this reaction may then react with atomic oxygen to regenerate NO.

$$NO_2 + O \rightarrow NO + O_2$$

The danger posed by NO is its capacity to destroy ozone molecules without being lost in the reaction.

> **Nitric oxide (NO) poses the most serious threat to the ozone layer of all nitrogen oxides.**

At one time, scientists were concerned about the threat NO posed to the ozone layer because of jet aircraft flying in the stratosphere and because of NO released by agricultural activities on Earth's surface. Today, these concerns have largely disappeared because of the more serious threat posed by a second class of compounds, the halogenated hydrocarbons.

Halogenated Hydrocarbons in the Ozone Layer

Halogenated hydrocarbons are organic compounds consisting of carbon, hydrogen, and one or more halogens. Halogenated hydrocarbons containing chlorine and fluorine are also known as chlorofluorocarbons (CFCs). Halogenated hydrocarbons containing chlorine and/or fluorine and at least one bromine atom are known as halons. The structures of some typical halogenated hydrocarbons are shown in Figure 12.

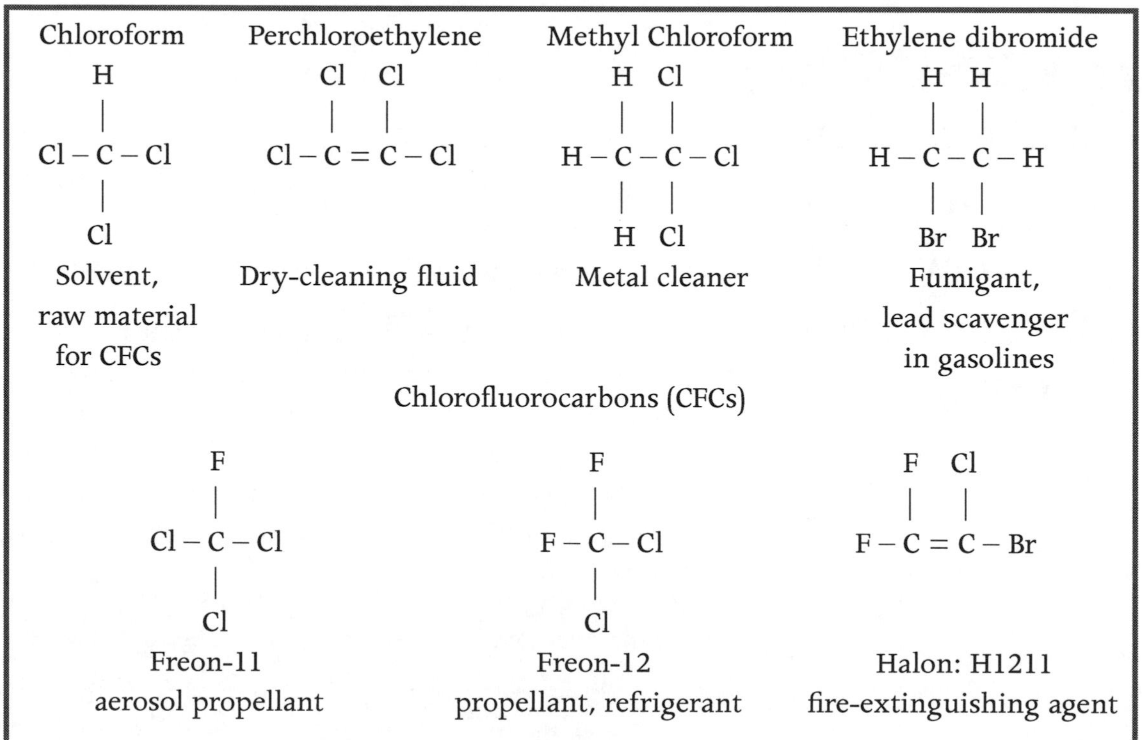

Figure 12

For many years, CFCs and halons have been extremely popular commercial compounds. They have been used in a wide variety of products from hair sprays to dry-cleaning fluids to refrigerants. One commercial advantage of these compounds is their stability.

Since they do not break down easily, they can be used for long periods of time without having to be replaced.

This stability is a mixed environmental blessing. On one hand, it means that toxic halogens will not readily be released to the environment when CFCs and halons decompose. On the other hand, once these compounds are released into the environment, they are likely to remain there for a very long time. They will also be able to migrate into the upper atmosphere before they decompose or undergo other chemical changes.

By the mid-1970s, some disturbing evidence regarding the use of CFCs and halons began to contradict this picture of relatively stable compounds. It seems that CFC and halon molecules that are stable in the troposphere become reactive in the stratosphere. Typically, ultraviolet radiation in the stratosphere causes the bonds in the CFC and halon molecules to break, resulting in the release of free halogen atoms. The following equation illustrates what can happen:

$$
\begin{array}{ccc}
\text{Cl} & & \text{Cl} \\
| & & | \\
\text{F} - \text{C} - \text{Cl} & \xrightarrow{h\nu} & \text{F} - \text{C}\cdot + \cdot\text{Cl} \\
| & & | \\
\text{F} & & \text{F}
\end{array}
$$

Once formed, the free halogen atom is available to attack ozone molecules, with the formation of chlorine oxide, ClO·.

$$Cl\cdot + O_3 \rightarrow ClO\cdot + O_2$$

This reaction is devastating to the ozone layer because it breaks down ozone, compounding the natural dissociation of ozone.

$$O_3 \rightarrow O + O_2$$

The ClO· formed in the reaction shown in the second equation is able to react with atomic oxygen—resulting from the natural breakdown of ozone—to regenerate the original chlorine atom.

$$ClO\cdot + O \rightarrow Cl\cdot + O_2$$

As a result, a single chlorine atom may be regenerated over and over again as a result of these reactions. By some estimates, one

> **Once formed, the free halogen atom is available to attack ozone molecules, with the formation of chlorine oxide, ClO·.**

chlorine atom may catalyze the decomposition of thousands of ozone molecules before it becomes part of a stable compound.

The most immediate concern about the loss of ozone is the effect it may have on skin cancer rates. Experts believe that each 1% decrease in stratospheric ozone may result in a 2% increase in the amount of ultraviolet radiation reaching the earth's surface. At low levels, the most serious consequence of increased levels of UV radiation is increased rates of skin cancer.

A 2% increase in UV radiation is thought to be responsible for a 2% to 5% increase in basal-skin cancer (often treated easily and successfully) and an 8% to 20% increase in squalmous-skin cancer (a more dangerous form of the disease). Given current skin cancer rates, these percentages could translate into 10,000 to 30,000 new cases of skin cancer each year in the United States.

> **Tracking changes in stratospheric ozone is a difficult task.**

The Antarctic Ozone Hole

Tracking changes in stratospheric ozone is a difficult task. It requires the ability to make precise measurements at altitudes of more than 50 kilometers and the unraveling of the chemical reactions that occur between species present in very low concentrations. As a result, for many years scientists were somewhat hesitant to say exactly what was happening to the ozone layer as a result of anthropogenic activities.

A very different situation began to develop in the mid-1980s, however. Studies showed that the concentration of ozone in a column above the South Pole had decreased by 40% in a single year. A review of existing records showed that a similar deficiency hole had been appearing each austral spring (September or October) as far back as 1979. Further studies conducted since 1985 have confirmed the reappearance of the ozone hole during each Antarctic spring.

The ozone hole reported in 1985 was enormous, covering an area of 40×10^6 km^2, about equal to the land area of the continental United States. Over the next decade, the ozone hole fluctuated in size but continued to grow nearly every year. In addition, a second hole in the ozone layer, this one over the Arctic, was discovered in 1989.

> **When the ozone hole over the Antarctic was first discovered, scientists were unsure of its precise cause.**

When the ozone hole over the Antarctic was first discovered, scientists were unsure of its precise cause. For about a decade, one of the prime suspects in the destruction of ozone in the stratosphere was CFCs released by human activities on the earth's surface. As early as 1974, two American scientists, Mario J. Molina and F. Sherwood Rowland, hypothesized a series of chemical reactions by which CFCs might be responsible for the destruction of atmospheric ozone. But in 1985, alternative explanations for the loss of ozone were still being considered. For example, some meteorologists suggested that changing weather conditions over the Antarctic might account for the dramatic changes in ozone concentration found above the South Pole.

This uncertainty created problems for industry and governmental agencies. If CFCs were responsible for the destruction of stratospheric ozone, then some regulatory action was needed to reduce the production of CFCs and their release into the atmosphere. If CFCs were *not* the culprit, industry and consumers would find themselves being asked to pay a huge price to create a solution that was not necessary.

Even before the discovery of the ozone hole, there was enough evidence about the involvement of CFCs for some governments to start placing restrictions on the production and use of CFCs. In 1979 the U.S. Environmental Protection Agency banned the use of CFCs in spray-can propellants, one of the many applications in which those compounds were used. A major problem confronting manufacturers, however, was that no satisfactory substitute for CFCs in most applications had been discovered.

The Montreal Protocol

An important turning point in efforts to save the ozone layer occurred in 1987. In that year, representatives from about 40 nations met in Montreal, Canada, to consider an agreement limiting the release of CFCs into the atmosphere. The document that was finally accepted, the *Montreal Protocol on Substances That Deplete the Ozone Layer,* called for a 50% cut in the use of CFCs by the year 2000. Within three years, 60 nations had endorsed the agreement. However, many less developed nations declined to take part in the accord. They feared that they could not afford to get along without, or find replacements for, the banned CFCs.

It was not long before scientists and government leaders realized how inadequate the Montreal Protocol was. Additional scientific evidence obtained after the 1987 meeting showed that ozone loss was occurring even more rapidly than scientists had speculated. World leaders met again in London in 1990 and in Copenhagen in 1992 to revise the Montreal agreement. At these meetings, agreements were reached to phase out all production of CFCs by 2000 (at the London meeting) and then by 1996 (at the Copenhagen meeting).

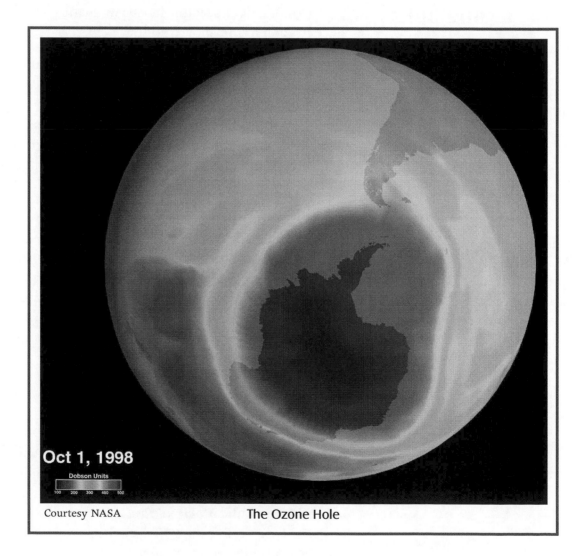

Oct 1, 1998

Dobson Units
100　200　300　400　500

Courtesy NASA　　　　The Ozone Hole

⊘ **EXPLORE**   **Exploration Activities**

1. How has the composition of the earth's atmosphere evolved since the planet's earliest days?

2. What is the process by which ozone is formed in the atmosphere?

3. Write a chemical equation that shows how nitric oxide depletes ozone in the stratosphere.

4. What is a halogenated hydrocarbon? How does a chlorofluorocarbon differ from a halogenated hydrocarbon?

5. Describe in chemical equations the series or reactions by which CFCs deplete ozone in the stratosphere.

BACKGROUND

Global Warming

The global environmental problem of most concern today involves a substance that is normally not even considered to be a pollutant: carbon dioxide. Recall that carbon dioxide is a normal component of air, the fourth most abundant gas in the atmosphere. The trouble is not the *presence* of CO_2 in the air but the apparent increase in the *amount* that is present.

Carbon dioxide enters and is removed from the atmosphere in a set of chemical reactions intimately involved with living organisms. The vast majority of plants manufacture new cellular material in the process known as photosynthesis. In photosynthesis, carbon dioxide and water are combined to produce cellulose and other complex carbohydrates.

> **In photosynthesis, carbon dioxide and water are combined to produce cellulose and other complex carbohydrates.**

$$CO_2 + H_2O \rightarrow (C_6H_{10}O_5)_x + O_2$$

In this equation, x is very large, usually in the hundreds or thousands.

Oxygen gas is a by-product of this reaction. In fact, photosynthesis is probably the primary reaction by which the earth's primitive atmosphere was converted from a reducing environment to an oxidizing environment rich in O_2.

Carbon dioxide is returned to the air during respiration, the process by which carbohydrates are oxidized to $CO_2 + H_2O$.

$$(C_6H_{10}O_5)_x + O_2 \rightarrow CO_2 + H_2O$$

This reaction is—at least in general form—the reverse of photosynthesis.

In nature, the rates at which CO_2 is produced and consumed are roughly equal. The concentration of CO_2 in the atmosphere as a result of natural processes changes by relatively small amounts.

Atmospheric CO_2 plays an important role in controlling the earth's mean temperature. Although the Earth obtains some heat from chemical and physical processes occurring within it, its main source of heat is solar energy. Sunlight consists of radiation of many wavelengths, including x-rays, ultraviolet light, visible light, and infrared radiation.

Most wavelengths of solar radiation are absorbed by substances in Earth's upper atmosphere. Stratospheric ozone, for example, absorbs ultraviolet radiation with wavelengths between about 200 and 280 nm. Visible light, with wavelengths ranging from about 400 to about 700 nm, is the only form of solar radiation that reaches the earth's surface in abundance. Figure 13 shows the relative amounts of radiation of each wavelength that reaches Earth's surface.

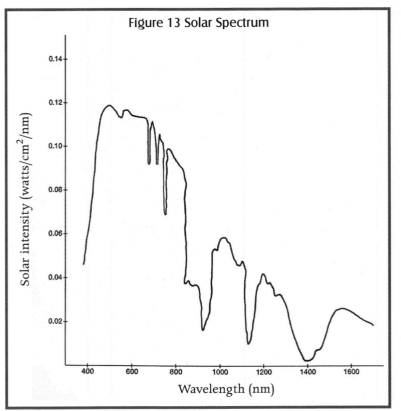

Figure 13 Solar Spectrum

About a third of the sunlight striking the earth's surface is reflected back into the atmosphere. The other two thirds is absorbed by rocks, soil, water, and other materials on the earth's surface. Absorption of visible light raises the temperature of these materials which, in turn, re-radiate energy to the atmosphere in the form of infrared radiation (heat) with wavelengths of 4,000 nm or more.

That portion of the re-radiated energy in the so-called near and far infrared regions ($\lambda = 4,000–8,000$ nm and >18,000 nm, respectively) is absorbed by water molecules, while that in the mid-infrared region ($\lambda = 13,000–18,000$ nm) is absorbed by CO_2 molecules. No atmospheric gas significantly absorbs radiation with wavelengths between 8,000 and 13,000 nm, so radiation of those wavelengths escapes into space. This last range of wavelengths is called the **atmospheric window.**

Earth's average annual temperature is another example of a steady-state system. Energy reaches the atmosphere in the form of solar radiation. That energy is converted at the earth's surface into infrared radiation, which is reflected back into the atmosphere.

There it is absorbed and retained by water and CO_2 molecules. Thus, water and CO_2 molecules constitute a kind of heat trap.

Some scientists see a similarity between this phenomenon and the process by which a greenhouse retains heat. They have, therefore, given the name "greenhouse effect" to the process of atmospheric warming.

Anthropogenic CO_2 and Global Climate Change

Human activities have had relatively little effect on the amount of CO_2 in the atmosphere until about the last hundred years. Since the mid-nineteenth century, however, human activities have had an increasing impact on CO_2 concentrations in the atmosphere. One reason for this change has been sheer numbers of humans. World population has increased from about 1 billion in about 1850, to about 2 billion around 1930, to about 3 billion in 1960, to about 4 billion in 1975, to more than 6 billion in 2003. Experts estimate that the planet will continue adding a billion more people every decade for the near future.

The more humans there are on Earth, the greater their impact on the environment. For example, as communities grow in population, forests are cut down to make more living space, to obtain land for farming, and to provide wood for fuel and construction. As forests are destroyed, a major sink for carbon dioxide is damaged, and more CO_2 escapes into the atmosphere.

The second factor affecting the increase in CO_2 production is the increasing technology available in most human communities. By far the most important element in that technology has been the use of fossil fuels. Since the 1850s, humans have been burning more and more coal, oil, and natural gas to heat homes and buildings, to power all forms of transportation, to generate electricity, and to operate factories.

To some extent, of course, the role of humans in this process is nothing other than as recyclers. The carbon dioxide produced during fossil fuel combustion may very well have been in the atmosphere previously, before it was incorporated into plants that eventually died, decayed, and turned into fossil fuels.

> **The more humans there are on Earth, the greater their impact on the environment.**

84

As a result of population growth and improvements in technology, the rate of CO_2 production from anthropogenic sources has been accelerating in the past half century. As Figure 14 shows, CO_2 emissions from all human activities between 1950 and 2000 have nearly tripled, from 1,640 to 5,800 million metric tons.

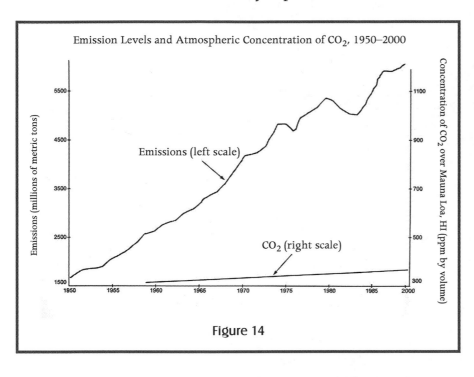

Emission Levels and Atmospheric Concentration of CO_2, 1950–2000

Figure 14

This trend appears to have resulted in an increase in the concentration of CO_2 in the atmosphere, as measured at two recording stations in Hawaii and the Antarctic. As Figure 14 also shows, however, the rate at which CO_2 concentrations in the atmosphere are increasing is much less than the rate at which CO_2 emissions are increasing from anthropogenic sources.

Effects of Changing CO_2 Concentrations

What significance does this data have for life on Earth? Scientists who can agree on the raw data summarized in Figure 14 dispute the meaning and significance of these trends. Some authorities see a cause-and-effect chain of events resulting from increasing levels of atmospheric CO_2, a chain that can be summarized as follows:

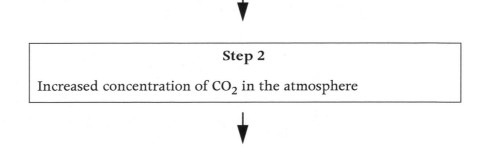

Step 1

Increased production of CO_2 from anthropogenic sources

Step 2

Increased concentration of CO_2 in the atmosphere

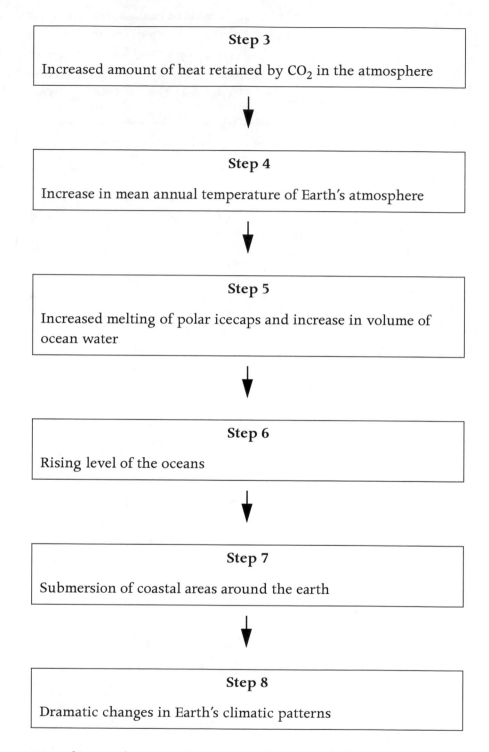

Step 3

Increased amount of heat retained by CO_2 in the atmosphere

Step 4

Increase in mean annual temperature of Earth's atmosphere

Step 5

Increased melting of polar icecaps and increase in volume of ocean water

Step 6

Rising level of the oceans

Step 7

Submersion of coastal areas around the earth

Step 8

Dramatic changes in Earth's climatic patterns

According to this scenario, even a relatively small increase in Earth's annual temperature (Step 4) could result in very large environmental changes. By one estimate, an increase in the mean annual temperature of 5°C would cause a rise in sea levels of 4.5 to 7.6 meters.

Temperature changes of this magnitude should be understood in the context of natural temperature variations in the earth's atmosphere. For example, a research group at the National Academy of Sciences (NAS) has estimated that the greatest temperature variations in Europe over the past 1,000 years has been about 1.5°C. NAS also estimated that the widest variation in the last 100,000 years—including the last Ice Age—was about 10°C.

> **The planet's temperature has gone up about 0.4°C in the past century.**

According to the best available estimates, the planet's temperature has gone up about 0.4°C in the past century. During the same time, the earth's oceans have risen by about 10 to 15 centimeters. Interpretations of these trends must also take into account the fact that the rate of CO_2 production, temperature increase, and rise in sea levels is expected to be significantly greater in the next few decades than it was in the past century.

In a 1983 study of possible greenhouse effects, NAS warned that one result of rising sea levels might be the danger they pose to coastal cities. Many of the world's great urban areas—Tokyo, New York City, Los Angeles, Boston, and London, for example—are located on or very near the ocean. An increase of only a few meters in sea level, NAS warned, could flood all or part of these cities. Low-lying areas everywhere might be drowned. According to the NAS study, a rise of 5 meters in sea level would submerge about a quarter of the state of Florida. In addition, a number of small island nations, such as Tuvalu, Kiribati, and the Maldives, might be entirely submerged. Two islands in the Kiribati archipelago, Tebua Tarawa and Abanuea, have already disappeared, apparently as a result of rising ocean levels.

The loss of polar icecaps might also have dramatic effects on the earth's climate (Step 8). Scientists have developed computer models to estimate some of these changes, but those models are not very precise so far. They do predict, in general, that productive farmlands in many parts of the world, such as those in the midwestern United States, may become too hot and dry to grow crops. At the same time, more northerly regions (such as Alaska and the Yukon) may become warm enough for year-round farming.

Other Anthropogenic Gases of Concern

Carbon dioxide is by no means the only greenhouse gas to cause concern. The term *greenhouse gas* is used to describe any gas that can absorb ultraviolet radiation re-radiated from the earth. For example, methane molecules absorb infrared radiation even more than CO_2 molecules do. Only the lower concentration of atmospheric methane makes this substance a less important consideration at the present time. However, if atmospheric temperatures continue to rise, decay of organic matter on Earth is likely to occur more rapidly, and methane, a product of that decay, may become even more abundant. By some estimates, the rate at which methane is being released to the environment is increasing even more rapidly than the rate of carbon-dioxide release.

Chlorofluorocarbons may also contribute to the greenhouse effect. Many of these compounds absorb infrared radiation in the region between 8,000 and 13,000 nm, in the range of the atmospheric window. This means that heat energy that normally escapes through the atmosphere's natural window is being trapped by CFCs. Therefore, the threat posed by CFCs is not that they are accelerating a natural process of heat retention, as is the case with CO_2, but that they are introducing a whole new mechanism for capturing and storing heat in the atmosphere.

> **The 1990s were the warmest decade ever recorded.**

Differences of Opinion

Stories in the popular media often present the possibility of global warming as if it were a settled issue. Such stories have been common over the past two decades as record-breaking temperatures have been recorded for the planet. For example, the nine hottest years ever recorded on the planet occurred in the 15-year period between 1987 and 2001. The 1990s were the warmest decade ever recorded. Such data have caused scientists, government officials, and ordinary citizens to ask whether global warming is in fact underway. And if it is, what consequences may be anticipated and what, if anything, can be done to slow down, stop, and ameliorate the effects of an enhanced greenhouse effect.

The problem is that global warming is an exceedingly complex and difficult issue. It does not lend itself to simple summaries, conclusions, and predictions, let alone simple solutions.

In fact, many scientists dispute the whole line of reasoning outlined in Steps 1 through 8 or at least doubt parts of the argument.

For example, a major point of contention seems to be the relationship between Steps 1 and 2. Until the mystery sink for CO_2—as illustrated in Figure 14—can be identified, no one can really determine what happens to all the carbon dioxide generated by anthropogenic sources (or, for that matter, carbon dioxide generated from any source).

Also, questions have been raised about the retention of heat in the earth's atmosphere. Perhaps there are natural processes, some critics say, through which excess heat is lost from the atmosphere. In that case, there would be no significant increase in the earth's annual mean temperature, and none of the following steps would occur.

A fundamental question involves the critical data on increases in the earth's annual mean temperature in the past. Some respected scientists have pointed out that most temperature readings are now made in urban areas. While it may be true that temperatures *have* increased in these areas—a point these scientists do not dispute—that does not necessarily mean that temperatures throughout the world have also increased. In fact, some studies show that the earth's annual mean temperature has actually decreased over the past 60 years.

Also, many factors not included in our eight-stage model may still have to be considered in assessing global warming. For example, a rise in the earth's annual average temperature should mean an increase in the rate of evaporation of water from the lithosphere and hydrosphere. That change might, in turn, result in an increase in the number and density of clouds in the atmosphere. But an increase in cloud volume and/or density could also mean that more solar radiation would be reflected back into space, producing an overall cooling effect.

According to this line of reasoning, the atmosphere may have a built-in self-correcting component. As temperatures rise and cloud cover increases, the amount of solar radiation reaching the earth's surface would decrease and temperatures would go back down. One scientist has calculated that a 1% increase in cloud density

> **Many factors not included in our eight-stage model may still have to be considered in assessing global warming.**

89

> At first glance, the destruction of forests would seem to be a contributing factor to global warming.

would reduce atmospheric temperature by as much as 0.5°C. At this point, scientists simply do not have enough data to know how important this effect might be in the atmosphere.

The effects of tropical rain forest destruction in global warming have also been discussed. At first glance, the destruction of these forests would seem to be a contributing factor to global warming. As more and more trees are cut down, the photosynthetic sink of CO_2 decreases in size. More carbon dioxide remains in the atmosphere and, presumably, atmospheric temperatures increase.

But we have very little data on this point. Some authorities point out that reforestation and the growth of new bushes and trees on abandoned farmlands are likely to increase the sink for carbon dioxide fairly rapidly. They think that the rate of increase may actually be greater than the loss of plant life as the result of deforestation. To the extent that this argument is valid, human activities might actually be contributing to a *decrease* in CO_2 concentrations in the atmosphere.

Controlling Greenhouse Gases

In spite of the number and variety of objections that have been raised to the eight-stage scenario, it seems almost certain that the vast majority of scientists who deal with environmental issues have come to the conclusion that human activities are altering the chemical composition of the earth's atmosphere, and that these changes will almost surely produce at least some significant environmental effects on the earth's climate.

These scientists, along with their allies in national and state governments and in many nongovernmental organizations, have been encouraging political leaders around the world for nearly two decades to begin taking steps to reduce the risk of global warming. Those steps could take one of two general forms: political actions or technological solutions (sometimes called technological fixes).

The most obvious political move that governments could make would be to require a reduction in the amount of CO_2 released to the atmosphere. They could require cutbacks in the amount of coal, oil, and natural gas burned in automotive vehicles, trains, ships, and airplanes; in industrial operations and power-generating plants; for the heating of homes and buildings; and for other purposes.

This option presents very significant challenges, however. In the first place, people would be required to accept a reduced standard of living: Smaller cars and fewer technological toys in developed nations, for example, and reduced access to electricity and fewer consumer products in developing nations. Also, some kind of international agreement would be needed, similar to the Montreal Protocol, in which all nations agree to cooperate in dealing with global climate change problems.

For many years, scientists and government officials despaired of ever reaching such an agreement. The price, in terms of reduced economic progress, was just too great, they feared, to gain environmental security. However, an effort to break through that impasse was made in Kyoto, Japan, in 1997, at a conference attended by representatives of 159 nations. After weeks of difficult bargaining, consensus was finally reached on a plan to reduce CO_2 emissions. The document that was eventually adopted at Kyoto called for reductions in carbon dioxide and other greenhouse gas emissions ranging from 6% below 1990 levels for Japan to 8% below those levels for members of the European Union. (The United States was assigned a 7% reduction.) The treaty was scheduled to go into effect when 55 nations accounting for at least 55 percent of all global carbon-dioxide emissions had ratified the treaty.

As of March 2003, 106 nations accounting for 43.9 percent of the world's carbon-dioxide emissions had ratified or accepted the treaty. Holdouts included a number of smaller nations, such as Liechtenstein, Monaco, and Saint Lucia, as well as some large nations with significant carbon-dioxide emission records, including Australia, Israel, the Russian Federation, Ukraine, and the United States.

Debate over treaty ratification was especially intense in the United States, where many observers felt that cutting back on emissions of carbon dioxide would produce a huge hardship on the economy. Americans were simply not willing, some politicians argued, to give up the kind of lifestyle to which they had become accustomed on the *chance* that the earth's climate might really be changing. Indeed, the official policy of three of the last four presidential

> **After weeks of difficult bargaining, consensus was finally reached on a plan to reduce CO_2 emissions.**

91

> **Some scientists have concluded that a political solution to the problem of global warming is simply not possible.**

administrations going back more than 20 years has been that too much uncertainty about the scientific basis for climate change remains, and that further research is necessary on the issue.

Some scientists have concluded that a political solution to the problem of global warming is simply not possible or that any such solutions will be inadequate. These experts have been looking for technological fixes that might reduce the enhanced greenhouse effect they believe is now taking place. For example, Dr. Thomas H. Stix, formerly a physicist at Princeton University, once suggested the use of laser beams to blast CFCs out of the stratosphere. The lasers would be tuned to wavelengths that CFCs absorb. The high energy of the laser beam might be enough to tear apart CFC molecules. Loss of CFC molecules would not only help protect the ozone layer, but it would also reopen the atmospheric window.

Another proposal for dealing with the problem of global warming has come from Dr. Wallace S. Broecker, professor of geochemistry at Columbia University. Dr. Broecker has suggested adding gases to the upper stratosphere that would increase the atmosphere's reflectivity. There is a natural precedent for this technique. When volcanoes erupt, they release millions of tons of ash to the atmosphere. The 1982 eruption of Mexico's El Chicon volcano, for example, produced a noticeable, if small, worldwide cooling in the following years. To produce this effect on an artificial scale, jumbo jets would have to carry millions of tons of some gas, such as sulfur dioxide, into the atmosphere.

Yet another approach involves the stimulation of phytoplankton growth in the oceans. Currently, the oceans serve as an important sink for atmospheric CO_2. Much of the carbon dioxide that dissolves in ocean water is absorbed and used by phytoplankton. Increasing the quantities of phytoplankton could also increase the rate at which CO_2 is removed from the atmosphere, some authorities believe.

Exploration Activities

1. By what two general processes is CO_2 added to and removed from the atmosphere?

2. What is the *atmospheric window,* and what is its importance to life on Earth?

3. Name three major human activities that contribute to the greenhouse effect.

4. What sequence of events is believed by some scientists to occur as a result of increasing CO_2 concentrations in the atmosphere?

5. Name two social and two technological solutions that have been proposed for the problem of global warming.

BACKGROUND

The Water Cycle

Water can be found in all three regions of the planet: atmosphere, lithosphere, and hydrosphere. Water vapor, for example, constitutes a small but important fraction of air, a fraction that varies widely from place to place on Earth. Water also occurs in the soil as groundwater. The movement of groundwater is an important process for both living organisms and natural geological events.

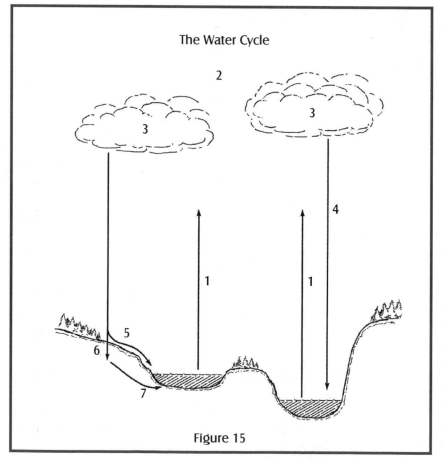

Figure 15

Water moves among the hydrosphere, atmosphere, and lithosphere in a process known as the **water cycle,** shown in Figure 15. At one stage of the cycle, water evaporates from lakes, rivers, oceans, and other parts of the hydrosphere (1). The water vapor becomes part of the atmosphere, either as dispersed water molecules (2) or condensed as tiny droplets of liquid water or ice crystals in clouds (3).

Dispersed water molecules eventually coalesce, condensing on particles of dust or other impurities in the air to form liquid droplets or tiny ice crystals (3). Droplets and crystals grow larger by accretion until they are heavy enough to fall back to Earth as precipitation (4). Precipitation may occur as rain, snow, hail, or sleet, depending on environmental conditions.

Some precipitation returns directly to the hydrosphere (4), completing the water cycle. Other precipitation falls on land (soil, vegetation, buildings, etc.) where it may run off the surface into a river or lake (5) or soak into the ground (6). Water that penetrates the soil becomes groundwater that slowly moves through the earth, returning to the hydrosphere and completing the water cycle (7).

Water is an excellent solvent that dissolves a variety of substances at every stage of the water cycle. All atmospheric gases are soluble to some extent in water. Thus, water that falls as rain is not completely pure but is a complex solution containing oxygen, nitrogen, carbon dioxide, and other trace gases. The pH of rainwater in equilibrium with atmospheric carbon dioxide is about 5.6.

Water in lakes, rivers, streams, and the oceans also dissolves atmospheric gases at the water's surface. Water also dissolves solids where it is in contact with riverbeds and lake and ocean bottoms. A stream that runs through a vein of limestone ($CaCO_3$), for example, will convert some of the calcium carbonate to a more soluble compound, calcium bicarbonate ($Ca(HCO_3)_2$).

$$CaCO_3(s) + H_2O(l) + CO_2(g) \rightarrow Ca(HCO_3)_2(aq)$$

As limestone dissolves, the stream loses some of its CO_2 and becomes less acidic.

> **Groundwater is especially efficient in dissolving minerals from the earth.**

Groundwater is especially efficient in dissolving minerals from the earth. When the process described in the equation above occurs deep underground, large blocks of limestone may be dissolved over long periods of time, resulting in the formation of caves. Once the cave is formed, groundwater dripping from its ceiling and onto its floor loses CO_2 to the air and water by evaporation. The equation is then driven to the left, calcium bicarbonate decomposes more rapidly, and calcium carbonate precipitates out of solution. The accumulation of $CaCO_3$ results in the formation of stalactites on cave ceilings and stalagmites on cave floors.

Anthropogenic chemicals in the atmosphere or lithosphere may become contaminants in the water cycle. To the extent that they pose a risk to living organisms, they may also be classified as pollutants. One example is the role of anthropogenic sulfur dioxide and nitrogen oxides in the production of acid precipitation. Also, pesticides and fertilizers used in agriculture may be dissolved by runoff or groundwater. We will focus on the most important anthropogenic pollutants found in the hydrosphere.

Exploration Activities

1. Outline the steps in the water cycle.

2. Why is rainwater acidic?

3. Why is groundwater a more efficient solvent of minerals than river water?

BACKGROUND

Types of Water Pollutants

Fouled stream banks, dead fish, oil-covered beaches, ponds filled with weeds, and smelly rivers are all evidence of polluted waters.

Some types of water pollutants are obvious to an observer. In some cases, animal wastes can be seen floating down a polluted stream. An oil slick on a lake is visible evidence of an accidental spill or intentional industrial discharge.

Yet, many types of water pollutants are not visible to the naked eye. Some of these pollutants are at least as hazardous to plant and animal life as the more visible forms. Table 9 lists some categories into which water pollutants may be grouped.

SOME TYPES OF WATER POLLUTANTS		
Pollutant	**Source(s)**	**Effects**
oxygen-demanding wastes	garbage; human and animal wastes	deprive aquatic organisms of oxygen
pathogens	human and animal wastes	cause disease
nutrients	fertilizers; agricultural and household wastes	lead to eutrophication of waterways
synthetic organic compounds	industry and agriculture; household and commercial detergents	toxic to aquatic and human life
petroleum products	household and industrial wastes	toxic to aquatic life; aesthetically displeasing
heavy metals	industrial and chemical processes	toxic to aquatic and human life
salts	agricultural, household, and industrial wastes	increase salinity; may be toxic
sediments	storm runoff and agricultural wastes	may clog waterways; may be harmful to aquatic organisms
acidity	mine and mine tailing runoffs; acid deposition	toxic to aquatic life
radioactive materials	military, industrial, chemical, and medical wastes	carcinogenic, teratogenic, and mutagenic
heat	power generation and industry	may be harmful to some forms of aquatic life

Table 9

 **Exploration Activities**

1. List six types of water pollutants.

2. What are some indicators of polluted water? What evidence of polluted water have you seen in your community?

Oxygen-Demanding Materials

Any body of water contains some waste organic materials. These materials might include dead plants, uneaten food from homes, and animal feces. Bacteria in the water oxidize (decompose) such materials to CO_2 and H_2O.

$$\text{organic material} + O_2 \xrightarrow{\text{bacteria}} CO_2 + H_2O.$$

Nitrogenous compounds in organic wastes, usually in the form of ammonium compounds, are also oxidized with the formation of nitrates.

$$NH_4^+ + 2O_2 \rightarrow NO_3^- + 2H^+ + H_2O$$

Oxidation is possible because of molecular oxygen dissolved in water. The amount of oxygen present in a sample of water depends on temperature and atmospheric pressure—that is, altitude. At sea level and 20°C, pure water holds 9.1 ppm of dissolved oxygen. At an altitude of 900 meters and a temperature of 20°C, the solubility of water is 8.2 ppm. And at the same altitude and a temperature of 40°C, its solubility drops to 5.8 ppm. (Recall that in water solutions, the unit *ppm* is comparable to a concentration expressed in milligrams per liter, or mg/L.)

> **The amount of oxygen present in a sample of water depends on temperature and atmospheric pressure.**

In an unpolluted river, stream, or lake, sufficient oxygen is available to decompose wastes and supply the needs of aquatic organisms. The water source becomes polluted when wastes accumulate and use up all or most of the dissolved oxygen in water. At that point, little or no dissolved oxygen remains in the water, and fish and other aquatic organisms begin to die.

One measure of the degree of pollution of water, therefore, is its **biochemical oxygen demand** (BOD), the amount of oxygen needed to decompose organic wastes in water. A high BOD value means that a large amount of oxygen is needed to oxidize a large volume of wastes, with little oxygen available to sustain aquatic life. A low BOD value means that only a small amount of oxygen is required to oxidize wastes, leaving sufficient oxygen for aquatic life.

99

SOME TYPICAL VALUES OF BIOCHEMICAL OXYGEN DEMAND	
Sample	**BOD (ppm)**
pure water	0
naturally occurring water	2–5
polluted water (when most fish begin to die)	>5
municipal sewage after primary and secondary treatment	10–20
untreated municipal sewage	100–400
runoff from barnyards and feedlots	100–10,000
wastes from food-processing plants	100–10,000

Table 10

The standard test for measuring BOD in a sample of water is to incubate the sample for five days at a temperature of 20°C. At the end of that period, the amount of oxygen consumed is measured, giving the BOD for that water sample. Some typical values of BOD are listed in Table 10.

Although BOD is the traditional method for measuring oxygen demand, other tests are also available. A much faster test is the **chemical oxygen demand** (COD) test. To measure COD, a sample of water is titrated against a strong oxidizing agent, typically potassium dichromate in sulfuric acid. The oxidizing agent performs the same function in the COD test of bacteria in the BOD test. The advantage of the COD test is that it produces results in a matter of hours, rather than days. The disadvantage of the test is that the oxidizing agent may oxidize materials that are not oxidized by bacteria, resulting in a slightly different assessment of the level of pollution of the water sample.

A third measure of oxygen demand is the **total organic carbon** (TOC) test. In this test, solids in a sample of water are collected and then burned at temperatures of about 1,000°C. The volume of CO_2 produced is measured, and from this value, the total mass of organic carbon in the sample can be determined. The TOC test can be completed in minutes.

Results obtained by these three tests are usually quite similar, but may differ since each measures a slightly different component of polluted water.

 **Exploration Activities**

1. Why are oxygen-demanding wastes pollutants?

2. What does the term *BOD* mean?

3. How does the COD test differ from the BOD test?

4. At what BOD level is water considered to be polluted?

BACKGROUND

Pathogens

Pathogens are disease-causing organisms. They may be viruses, bacteria, protozoa, parasitic worms, or other microorganisms. The most important source of pathogens in water is wastes from infected humans and other animals. A person infected with cholera, for example, expels cholera bacteria in her or his feces and urine. Those bacteria may then enter a public water supply and be passed on to other humans.

At one time, waterborne pathogens were a major health problem throughout the world. The desire to prevent diseases such as typhoid fever, dysentery, polio, and infectious hepatitis was, in fact, the primary reason for early campaigns to introduce pollution control systems in public water supplies. The use of chlorination in water treatment plants today destroys virtually all pathogenic organisms. Thus, waterborne pathogens are seldom a problem in the more developed nations of the world.

That is not the case in many less developed areas, however. The majority of humans alive today do not have access to purified water, as is the case in industrialized nations. As a result, diseases such as cholera, typhoid fever, salmonellosis, shigellosis, hepatitis A, amoebic dysentery, gastroenteritis, and giardiasis still cause millions of deaths worldwide each year.

A simple test used to estimate pathogens in water involves a count of the number of **coliform bacteria** present in a water sample. Coliform bacteria are harmless microorganisms that live in the human digestive tract. Each person excretes millions or billions of coliform bacteria every day. A person infected with a pathogen will excrete both coliform bacteria and pathogens.

To estimate the concentration of pathogens in water, a count is made of the number of coliform bacteria present in a sample of water. The number of bacteria present indicates the amount of fecal matter discharged into the water. Since the bacteria die quickly in water, the count indicates how long it has been since the fecal matter entered the water. Then, from the concentration of coliform bacteria in the water sample, a rough estimate of the concentration of pathogens can be made.

> **The majority of humans alive today do not have access to purified water.**

102

> **Coliform bacteria may originate in sources other than the human intestinal tract.**

A distinction is made between **total coliform count** and **fecal coliform count.** Coliform bacteria may originate in sources other than the human intestinal tract. For example, some coliform bacteria feed on decaying vegetable matter. The number of coliform bacteria that originate exclusively from the human digestive system—the fecal coliform count—provides a more accurate assessment of the probable number of pathogens present in a water sample. Fecal coliforms can be distinguished from nonfecal coliforms because of the way they ferment a certain form of sugar, lactose, at the temperature of $44.5°C$.

The U.S. Environmental Protection Agency has established an upper limit of 2.2 coliform bacteria per 100 mL of drinking water. Higher concentrations (200 coliform bacteria per 100 mL) are permitted for aquatic activities, such as fishing, boating, and swimming.

 **Exploration Activities**

1. Why are waterborne pathogens a major health problem in less developed regions of the world?

2. Why are coliform bacteria used to measure the level of pathogens in water?

BACKGROUND

Organic Compounds

Over the last half century, chemists have discovered and invented millions of organic compounds. Environmental chemists sometimes refer to such compounds as **synthetic organic compounds** (SOCs). The vast majority of these compounds do not exist in nature, and we know little or nothing about their effects on humans, other animals, plants, and the physical environment, or about their fates in the environment.

Synthetic organic compounds are found in a wide variety of places. The chemicals used to make detergents, pesticides, paint, plastic soda bottles, fingernail polish, and many types of clothing material, such as Dacron, nylon, and polyester, are all SOCs. Synthetic motor oil, brake fluid, and transmission fluid contain SOCs, as do some medicines, candles, artificial scents, and artificial flavorings for a variety of foods.

Many SOCs possess two characteristics that make them a potential risk to the environment. First, they tend to be highly stable. As synthetic compounds, they are likely to be unaffected by microorganisms that decompose naturally occurring substances. Also, in many cases, they tend to be toxic to plant and/or animal life.

These two characteristics mean that once an SOC is released into the environment, there is some probability that it will become part of a food chain, accumulate in the upper levels of that chain, and eventually have harmful effects on members of that chain.

We will focus on two members of that category that have been studied fairly thoroughly: synthetic detergents and pesticides.

 **Exploration Activities**

1. List at least five things you use every day that contain SOCs.

2. What two characteristics make SOCs a potential threat to the environment?

BACKGROUND

Synthetic Detergents

The term **detergent** applies to any substance that acts as a cleaning agent. In human history, the most important detergent has been soap. As the product of naturally occurring fats and oils, soaps biodegrade easily and pose little hazard to the environment.

The products known as **synthetic detergents,** or *syndets,* are complex mixtures with cleaning properties similar to those of natural soaps. Among the components of a modern syndet are a **surfactant,** a **builder,** a brightener, an antifoaming agent, artificial odor, antiredeposition agents, bleaches, and enzymes.

The structural formulas for a typical soap and a typical surfactant molecule are shown in Figure 16. Notice that both molecules consist of long chains, one end of which is ionic and the other covalent. In each molecule, the ionic end of the chain is attracted to water, while the covalent end is attracted to organic groups, such as those found in fats and oils.

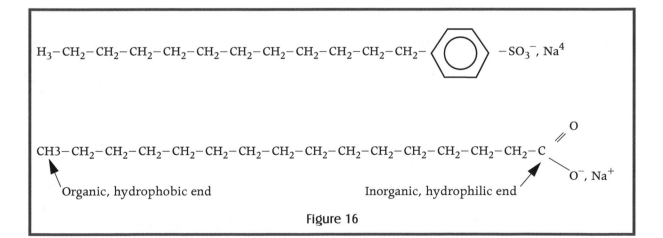

Figure 16

Such molecules are effective cleaning agents because they act as emulsifying agents between water and oil-covered droplets of dirt found on clothing, soiled dishes, and dirty hands and faces. Figure 17 shows that happens on a molecular level when a soap or syndet is mixed with dirt particles found in the water. The roughly spherical particle formed by the process, consisting of about 100 detergent molecules, is called a *micelle.*

Natural soap and some kinds of syndets do not work well in certain kinds of water. These kinds of water contain Ca^{2+}, Mg^{2+}, Fe^{2+}, Fe^{3+}, and other ions often present in the ground. Water that contains such ions is said to be hard, because it is difficult to produce soap suds using the water.

Hardness in water is caused by the fact that these dissolved ions react with a portion of the detergent molecule to form a precipitate. A typical reaction is the following:

$$2C_{17}H_{35}COO^- + Na^+(aq) + Ca^{2+}(aq) \rightarrow Ca(C_{17}H_{35}COO)_2(s) + Na^+(aq)$$

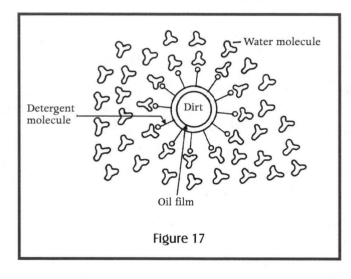

Figure 17

The precipitate formed in this reaction is a gummy, gray material, perhaps most familiar as the ring that forms in a bathtub. It tends to collect on clothing and other objects that are washed in hard water.

Hard water can be used for washing, but not very efficiently. Soap added to hard water first reacts with metal ions in the water, as shown in the equation above. After all metallic ions have been deposited, additional soap is then available for cleaning.

Another way of dealing with the ions that cause hardness in water is to use builders. Builders are sequestrants that remove ions such as Ca^{2+}, Mg^{2+}, Fe^{2+}, and Fe^{3+} from water. One of the most efficient builders yet discovered is sodium tripolyphosphate (TPP), $Na_5P_3O_{10}$. The sequestering agent in this compound is the cation $P_3O_{10}^{5-}$, which binds to metallic ions to form soluble complexes. The charged $CaP_3O_{10}^{3-}(aq)$ ion bonds to water molecules and remains in solution. One of the best known commercial forms of a builder is the water softener known as Calgon™ (*calcium gone*).

Detergents and Eutrophication

Syndets may pose an environmental hazard largely because of the builders they contain. Probably the most significant of these hazards is the increased rate of eutrophication of lakes and ponds. **Eutrophication** is a natural process by which a lake or pond evolves into dry land.

> **As the concentration of nutrients in the lake increases, the growth of aquatic plants and animals accelerates.**

When a lake or pond is young, it contains few dissolved materials. Plant and animal growth in the lake is slow because the water lacks the nutrients organisms need. Over time, these nutrients are carried into the lake or pond by rains, streams, and groundwater. As the concentration of nutrients in the lake increases, the growth of aquatic plants and animals accelerates.

Two essential nutrients for plants are nitrogen and phosphorus. Over a period of time, the accumulation of these nutrients increases the rate of plant growth. Eventually, the lake becomes clogged with plants, and aquatic organisms begin to die off. The body of water evolves from a lake or pond into a swamp or bog and eventually into a meadow.

Under natural conditions, in the absence of human activity, eutrophication takes place in most lakes and ponds. But the process normally takes thousands or millions of years. Human activities may greatly accelerate the rate at which eutrophication occurs, so that some lakes complete the process in hundreds or even dozens of years.

For example, fertilizers washed off farmlands contain compounds of both nitrogen and phosphorus. Runoff from pasture land may also contain nitrogen and phosphorus compounds from animal wastes deposited on the land. In addition, untreated domestic sewage contains human wastes that are rich in both of these nutrients.

The builders in syndets are yet another major anthropogenic source of phosphorus. In some areas, half the phosphorus contained in sewage comes from detergents. The accumulation of phosphorus in lakes from detergents and other anthropogenic sources is of great concern because phosphorus is often the limiting factor in the eutrophication process.

The term **limiting factor** refers to the condition that controls the growth or abundance of an organism or group of organisms. In many aquatic systems, carbon, hydrogen, oxygen, and nitrogen are available in abundance to organisms. Of all major nutrients, phosphorus may be the least readily available. Thus, the concentration of phosphorus in a lake may be the limiting factor that regulates the rate at which organisms grow.

In the absence of human activity, little phosphorus is washed into lakes, and organisms tend to grow slowly. In the presence of farming, urban growth, and other human activities, the release of phosphorus increases rapidly. As a consequence, the rate of eutrophication may be accelerated greatly.

Concern about this effect has prompted many states to ban or limit the use of polyphosphates in syndets. Detergent manufacturers have raised questions about such legislation, however. First, they have been unable to find other compounds that work as efficiently as builders. The manufacturers have investigated the use of compounds such as sodium carbonate (Na_2CO_3), borates, and carboxymethylcellulose, but without much success so far.

The most promising substitute for polyphosphates at this point appears to be the sodium salt of nitrilotriacetic acid, $3Na^+$, $N(CH_2CO_2)_3^-$, or NTA. But NTA is of concern to environmentalists because of data indicating that the compound may be carcinogenic in rats. The U.S. Environmental Protection Agency banned the use of NTA in detergents in 1970, and then changed its mind and once more permitted the use of NTAs in 1980.

The mechanism by which NTA sequesters metal ions is shown here:

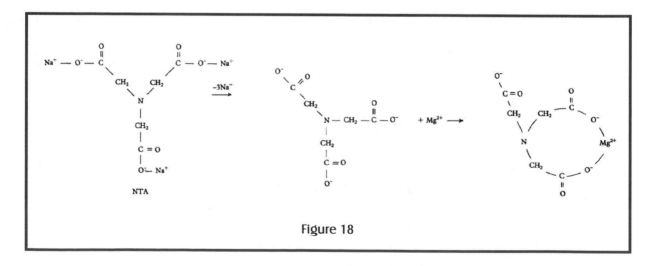

Figure 18

Detergent manufacturers also question the extent to which polyphosphates actually contribute to eutrophication. Plant growth requires carbon and nitrogen in addition to phosphorus.

110

> **Manufacturers claim that removal of phosphates from detergents will not necessarily guarantee that accelerated eutrophication of water sources will slow down or stop.**

Research has shown that any one of these nutrients can act as the limiting factor in controlling plant growth under any one set of environmental conditions. Manufacturers claim that removal of phosphates from detergents will not necessarily guarantee that accelerated eutrophication of water sources will slow down or stop.

Finally, manufacturers point out that phosphates are successfully removed in the tertiary treatment of wastewater. As expensive as tertiary treatment is, the country might be better served spending its money there rather than on further research into substitutes for the highly efficient polyphosphates, they claim.

The issue of detergent-driven eutrophication has not yet been entirely solved in the United States and many other parts of the world. Following vigorous debates about the problem in the 1970s, a number of cities, states, and regional governments enacted bans on the use of polyphosphates in detergents, at least for some purposes and in some locations. But the products were still allowed for certain uses, such as industrial, commercial, and hospital purposes. This patchwork system remains in effect today, with no consistent national policy having been adopted by the U.S. government.

Concerns about the issue appear, for the most part, to have largely disappeared from the public consciousness. Seldom does one read in the newspapers about the problem of eutrophication resulting from the use of polyphosphate-based detergents. Yet, many environmental chemists believe that nutrient pollution continues to be the number-one water quality problem worldwide.

Exploration Activities

1. How are soap and surfactant molecules structurally similar?

2. By what mechanism do soaps and syndets remove dirt from objects?

3. What is the function of a builder in a syndet?

4. How does the use of syndets contribute to eutrophication of lakes?

BACKGROUND

Pesticides

Insects, birds, rodents, and other animals have always competed with humans for food. In some parts of the world, it is not unusual for one third to half of a farmer's crop to be lost to pests, either in the field or during storage of harvested crops. Weeds also compete with crops for space, air, light, and nutrients. Thus, human farmers have been doing battle with other animals and plants for their crops since the beginning of agriculture.

Until the 1950s, farmers had two weapons to use in this battle: natural pesticides found in plants (such as pyrethrum) and minerals containing arsenic, lead, and mercury. Then, following World War II, chemists began to develop a number of SOCs for use as pesticides and herbicides.

<table>
<tr><td colspan="3" align="center">SOME CATEGORIES OF PESTICIDES,
CLASSIFIED ACCORDING TO THEIR USE</td></tr>
<tr><th>Category</th><th>Target</th><th>Example</th></tr>
<tr><td>avicide</td><td>birds</td><td>ornitrol</td></tr>
<tr><td>bactericide</td><td>bacteria</td><td>bacitracin</td></tr>
<tr><td>fungicide</td><td>fungi</td><td>Dinoseb</td></tr>
<tr><td>insecticide</td><td>insects</td><td>parathion</td></tr>
<tr><td>larvicide</td><td>larvae</td><td>Zectran</td></tr>
<tr><td>molluscicide</td><td>snails and slugs</td><td>mataldehyde</td></tr>
<tr><td>nematicide</td><td>roundworms</td><td>1,3-dichloropropene</td></tr>
<tr><td>rodenticide</td><td>rodents</td><td>warfarin</td></tr>
<tr><td>herbicide</td><td>plants</td><td>paraquat</td></tr>
</table>

Table 11

These products can be classified according to their use or according to their chemical structures. Tables 11 and 12 illustrate both methods of classification.

The use of SOCs as pesticides and herbicides has revolutionized modern agriculture. Food production in the last 40 years has doubled in the more developed countries and has increased by 120% in the less developed countries. A large fraction of those increases has come about because of the use of SOCs as pesticides, herbicides, and chemical fertilizers. These chemicals have made a substantial contribution to solving the world's hunger problem and maintaining a high standard of living in the more developed countries.

SOME CATEGORIES OF PESTICIDES, CLASSIFIED ACCORDING TO THEIR CHEMICAL STRUCTURES

Class	Example	Chemical Formula	Use
chlorinated hydrocarbons	DDT		insecticide
halogenated hydrocarbons	dibromo-chloropropane		nematicide
organophosphates	parathion		insecticide
chlorophenoxy acids	2,4,5-T		herbicide
carbamates	Carbaryl (Sevin)		molluscicide and larvicide
triazines	atrazine		herbicide
dithiocarbamates	Nabam		fungicide
organic salts	sodium fluoroacetate		rodenticide
dinitrophenols	Dinoseb		herbicide

Table 12

Unfortunately, the use of pesticides has been accompanied by a number of environmental problems. For example, the use of chemical pesticides often results in the development of more resistant strains of pests. During the first use of a pesticide, the vast majority of organisms will be killed off. But the small fraction that remain will consist of the most hardy individuals.

When these individuals breed, they will produce a second generation that, overall, will be more resistant to the pesticide than the first generation. A second use of the pesticide will produce a similar result in the third generation, a population of individuals that are even more resistant to the pesticide.

> **Over many generations, a larger and larger fraction of individuals will survive treatment by the pesticide.**

Over many generations, a larger and larger fraction of individuals will survive treatment by the pesticide. The pesticide will become less and less effective. As a consequence, farmers will want to use more and more of it to achieve results comparable to those of earlier use. Excess pesticide will wash off into the soil, groundwater, and surface waters, and will become airborne, posing a number of environmental risks.

Those risks result from the characteristics of SOCs in general: persistence and toxicity. Most pesticides and herbicides are, after all, poisons. The aim of a chemist who is designing a new pesticide or herbicide is to produce a chemical that will kill a specific type or class of pests or weeds, but that will not be too toxic for desired plants and animals. Rapid decomposition in the environment is also a highly desirable characteristic of a new pesticide. When compounds with these characteristics are discovered, they are valuable contributions to agricultural science.

The DDT Story

Pesticides are often toxic to a wide range of organisms, including many that are not pests, and/or the pesticide will remain in the environment for months or years. This was the case with perhaps the most famous pesticide of all, a compound by the name of dichlorodiphenyltrichloroethane, or DDT.

DDT was first synthesized in 1874, but it was essentially forgotten for more than 60 years. Then, in 1939 the Swiss chemist Paul Mueller found that DDT was highly toxic to insects. Almost immediately, the Swiss government began to use DDT against a major local pest, the Colorado potato beetle. The new pesticide turned out to be highly effective.

Within two decades, DDT was a spectacular success on many fronts. It was used in agriculture against insect pests and by medical workers against disease-carrying organisms. It was instrumental in increasing yields of many crops and in reducing death rates from a number of diseases.

The problem was that DDT was both persistent and toxic. The persistence of a chemical in the environment can be measured by its **half-life**. The half-life of a substance is defined as the time it takes for the concentration of that substance to be reduced by half in some biological system. For example, the half-life of DDT in soil ranges from three to 10 years. Half-lives for any one substance vary because of temperature, humidity, and other factors. Thus, a single application of DDT might survive at measurable levels for a generation or more.

Also, DDT is soluble in fats. When an organism ingests DDT, the pesticide concentrates in fatty parts of the organism's body. If the organism is eaten by another organism, the DDT is passed along to the predator from the prey. At the same time, DDT is not readily metabolized by most organisms. Thus, it is not changed into a water-soluble form that can be excreted.

As a result, the concentration of DDT found in organisms in a food chain increases as it moves up the chain. In one study, a concentration of 5×10^{-5} ppm was found in the water of a salt marsh, a concentration of 4×10^{-2} ppm in plankton living in that water, a concentration of 0.2 to 1.2 ppm in small fish that fed on the plankton, a concentration of 1 to 2 ppm in large fish that ate the smaller fish, and a concentration of 3 to 76 ppm in fish-eating birds at the top of this food chain.

This phenomenon of **biological magnification** is applicable for any substance, such as an SOC, that does not decompose readily in the environment. Two additional necessary conditions for this process are that the substance be (1) ingested by organisms but (2) not excreted by them. When such substances are also toxic, their threat to living organisms becomes obvious.

In the case of DDT, scientists began to notice many environmental problems resulting from the use of the pesticide. For example,

> **A single application of DDT might survive at measurable levels for a generation or more.**

some animals no longer reproduced normally. Birds at the top of food chains laid eggs with unusually thin shells, so the chicks could not develop normally. Other animals were born with deformities, while some died outright as a result of DDT poisoning.

Even given the advantages of DDT as an agricultural and public health tool, the U.S. Environmental Protection Agency decided in 1973 to ban its use in nearly all applications. As an indication of the pesticide's persistence in the environment, however, a 1986 study showed an average level of 1.67 ppm of DDT in the fatty tissue of humans, more than 10 years after the compound had been banned from general use.

The DDT story has never had a simple beginning and end. The fact is that the pesticide has always been very successful, which, despite its effects on some animals, has never been implicated in the death of a single human. Although DDT was banned as early as the 1960s in some parts of the world, it has remained in use for at least some purposes in many other regions.

> **Many nations have continued to permit the use of DDT for the spraying of mosquito-infested areas.**

One of the most important purposes for which it has been used is in spraying for the *Anopheles* mosquito that is responsible for the transmission of malaria. Malaria is one of the world's primary causes of death, killing about 2.5 million people every year. Many nations have continued to permit the use of DDT for the spraying of mosquito-infested areas because the risk to the biological environment of the pesticide was determined to be less than the risk of the mosquitoes to humans.

As an example of the compound's effectiveness, the number of cases of malaria was reduced from more than 8 million in 1943 in Venezuela to 800 in 1958. Similar results were obtained in Italy, where the number of malaria cases dropped from 411,502 in 1945 to 37 in 1968, and in Taiwan, where the rate dropped from over 1 million in 1945 to just nine in 1969.

These results have prompted many public health scientists to call for a reconsideration of bans on the use of DDT for the spraying of mosquitoes. For example, a group called Save Children from Malaria Campaign pointed out in 2000 that ending spraying programs almost inevitably resulted in a new increase in the spread of malaria. The group's concerns were expressed just as the United Nations Environment Programme was announcing an international

> **DDT is certainly not the only SOC pesticide and herbicide about which environmental concerns have been expressed.**

agreement to end the production of 12 SOC pesticides, DDT among them.

As the UN action indicates, DDT is certainly not the only SOC pesticide and herbicide about which environmental concerns have been expressed. Some of the other products that either have already been banned or that are candidates for such bans include the pesticides and herbicides called aldrin, chlordane, dieldrin, endrin, heptachlor, hexachlorobenzene, Mirex, and toxaphene.

Alternatives to SOC Pesticides

How can science continue to provide new products for use in agriculture and public health, like the SOCs that have already been invented, that will increase the efficiency of crop growth and health protection? One answer is to keep inventing new SOCs, new compounds that may be as effective as those that have been banned but that are less hazardous to the environment. Many organic chemists are engaged in this kind of research today.

Another approach is to find alternative methods of pest control. Some possibilities include the following.

- *Biological controls:* Natural enemies of a pest are introduced into the field. These enemies—viruses, bacteria, fungi, insects, etc.—destroy the pests by natural means through a predator–prey relationship.

- *Sterilization techniques:* Adult members of a pest population are sterilized—for example, with low levels of radiation—and then released into the field. When sterile adults mate with normal adults, no offspring are produced.

- *Resistant plants:* New strains of crops are developed that are genetically resistant to certain pests. These plants do not require as much, or any, pesticide spraying.

- *Hormone control:* Hormones that occur naturally in a pest can be synthesized in the laboratory and sprayed on the field. These hormones interrupt the normal development of pests and prevent them from becoming adults.

The debate over how best to control pests and weeds is a vigorous one today.

- *Sex attractants:* Female insects release certain chemicals called pheromones to indicate that they are ready to breed. Chemists can synthesize these pheromones and use them to bait traps in which to capture pests.

The debate over how best to control pests and weeds is a vigorous one today. In addition to the scientific considerations mentioned here, economics is an important factor. The production of SOCs is a highly profitable enterprise for chemical companies. At this point, it is not clear that alternative methods of pest control would be as profitable. Thus, decisions about pesticide and herbicide use often focus as much on corporate profits as on scientific and technological issues.

119

Exploration Activities

1. Name five categories of pesticides according to their function, and name the pest against which each category is used.

2. List the advantages and disadvantages of DDT as a pesticide.

3. To what does the term *biological magnification* refer?

4. Describe two methods of pest control that do not use SOCs.

BACKGROUND

Petroleum Products

Oil spills are one of the most dramatic examples of environmental damage. In March 1989, for example, the oil tanker *Exxon Valdez* ran aground in Alaska's Prince William Sound. The tanker broke open and released about 44 million liters (45,000 metric tons) of crude oil into the sound. An oil slick covered hundreds of square kilometers of the sound, oil began washing up on shore, and aquatic life and birds became ill and died.

Probably the most interesting point is that big, attention-getting accidents like the *Valdez* spill constitute only a minor portion of the estimated 2 million to 5 million metric tons of oil released into the environment each year. By one estimate, 85% of the petroleum products that get into the hydrosphere come from other sources. The most important of these sources are the following.

> **Individuals and industries everywhere are most likely to dump their petroleum waste into the nearest sewer or river.**

- *Used industrial and motor oils:* U.S. law prohibits the dumping of oil into sewage systems or waterways. Still, few communities provide systems for the collection of these wastes. Most other nations of the world do not even have laws regulating petroleum waste disposal. As a result, individuals and industries everywhere are most likely to dump their petroleum waste into the nearest sewer or river. About 56% of the petroleum products discharged into rivers, lakes, and oceans comes from these sources.

- *Normal shipping operations:* All ships—not just oil tankers— carry some oil for fuel, lubrication, and other purposes. A portion of this oil inevitably escapes the ship's hull, sometimes by accident and sometimes intentionally.

Oil tankers do present a special problem, however. After a tanker has delivered oil to its destination, it takes on seawater as ballast. The seawater goes into the same tanks that carry oil. When the tanker takes on another load of oil, it must pump out the seawater ballast, now mixed with some oil, into the ocean.

Large and small accidents, such as the one involving the *Exxon Valdez,* are yet another type of shipping-related petroleum discharge. Although any one such incident can be a local disaster, the much more frequent worldwide release from everyday shipping operations is generally a more serious concern. The loss of petroleum products from tankers and other ships in all types of incidents is thought to account for about 20% of all oil in the hydrosphere.

- *Natural leaks:* Oil constantly escapes the earth's mantle through cracks and holes in the ocean floor. About 15% of the world's oil pollution comes from this source.

- *Offshore production:* An increasing fraction of the petroleum produced around the world comes from offshore wells. When accidents occur at such wells, oil is released directly into the ocean. A Mexican oil well in the Gulf of Mexico blew out in 1979, releasing 11 million liters (10,000 metric tons) of crude oil over a nine-month period. Oil, dead birds, and fish washed up on Texas beaches, more than 6,000 kilometers away.

Accidents such as this one, combined with the daily loss of oil during normal operations from offshore wells, produce about 5% of the world's total oil pollution of the hydrosphere.

> **Oil, dead birds, and fish washed up on Texas beaches, more than 6,000 kilometers away.**

Oil-Water Interactions in an Oil Spill

Exactly how oil affects the environment is not well understood. To begin with, petroleum is a very complex mixture. Various components of petroleum exert various effects on organisms in the environment.

By far the most common constituents of petroleum are hydrocarbons. It is not uncommon for a single sample of petroleum to contain 150 to 175 different hydrocarbons. Roughly half of these hydrocarbons are aliphatic and half aromatic.

No single compound makes up more than about 2% of a sample. Typically, alkanes with 7 to 14 percent carbon atoms predominate. The most common alkanes encountered are n-hexane (C_6H_{14}), n-heptane (C_7H_{16}), n-octane (C_8H_{18}), n-nonane (C_9H_{20}), and n-decane ($C_{10}H_{22}$). These alkanes appear in concentrations of about 1% to 2%, by weight. Some of the aromatics found in petroleum include benzene (C_6H_6), toluene (C_7H_8), and three isomers of xylene (C_8H_{10}). Even the most abundant of the aromatics occur in concentrations of less than 1%.

> **When oil is spilled on water, several physical and chemical changes begin to occur.**

Other elements also occur in small concentrations in petroleum. These include sulfur (less than 0.1% to about 5%), nitrogen (0.1% to about 2%), and oxygen (0.1% to about 2%). Also, certain heavy metals, such as iron (up to 30 ppm), nickel (up to 50 ppm), vanadium (up to 50 ppm), and copper (up to 1 ppm), occur in the form of organic compounds.

When oil is spilled on water, several physical and chemical changes begin to occur. Among these are evaporation, dispersion ("flushing"), emulsification, coagulation, dissolving, and oxidation. Each of these processes is described briefly below.

- *Evaporation:* A significant fraction of any petroleum sample is highly volatile and will evaporate within a few days. By this process, up to a quarter of the spill is removed rapidly. Of course, this means that the volatile compounds have become part of the atmosphere.

- *Dispersion:* Oil is only slightly soluble in water and is less dense. Immediately after a spill, oil will spread out in a thin layer on the surface of the water. This process—also called *flushing*—insures that the area of contact between oil and water will be very large, increasing the likelihood of chemical interactions between the components of these otherwise immiscible liquids.

- *Emulsification:* The churning action of waves tends to break down the oil slick into tiny droplets that are then emulsified with water droplets. Emulsified oil is then dispersed throughout the whole body of water. Water droplets may also become trapped within larger oil droplets. When these droplets collide and accumulate, they may produce a sticky, tar-like mass that floats on the surface of the water.

- *Coagulation:* Petroleum may contain dense, tarry fractions that tend to collect and coagulate. As these masses become larger, they may form clumps or mats of tarry, asphalt-like materials that wash up on shore. Droplets and particles formed by emulsification and/or coagulation may contain enough heavy ions to cause them to sink to the ocean bottom.

- *Dissolving:* Oil and water are said to be immiscible. Yet some components of petroleum are at least slightly soluble in water. This means that some fraction, even if small, of petroleum will dissolve in water. The large surface area of the oil-water interface and the churning action of waves tend to increase the rate at which these slightly soluble compounds dissolve.

- *Oxidation:* Hydrocarbons that do not evaporate, settle out on the ocean bottom, or deposit on the shore are likely to be oxidized. Oxidation may occur photolytically, that is, as the result of solar energy. More commonly, these hydrocarbons are oxidized by microorganisms. In either case, the major products of oxidation are CO_2 and H_2O.

Environmental Effects of Oil Spills

Once dispersed in water, petroleum affects organisms in a variety of ways. Many of the components of oil are toxic. These components tend to kill organisms outright. Benzene, toluene, xylene, naphthalene, and phenanthrene are examples of such compounds. One of the first effects of a spill, therefore, is the rapid death of fish, shellfish, and aquatic invertebrates.

Toxic substances in oil can cause other effects. For example, sea otters may develop nosebleeds or emphysema, or they may be blinded by oil. Damage to their livers and kidneys may disable the otters and eventually lead to their deaths. Animals not directly harmed by a spill may also be affected. Bears and river otters, for example, may scavenge on seabirds killed by the spill. Toxins in the birds may then exert a secondhand effect on these mammals.

Over a longer period, microorganisms may also die off as a result of oxygen depletion. As oxygen is used up in the oxidation of petroleum, less is available for aerobic microorganisms in the area.

Some of the effects of an oil spill most obvious to the general public result from the purely physical effect of coating by oil. Oil may soak into a bird's feathers or a mammal's fur, for example, destroying the natural insulating and weatherproofing properties of feathers and fur. As a result, these animals may drown or die of exposure.

Oil slicks may also cover aquatic plants, algae, and lichen, depriving these organisms of carbon dioxide and oxygen, and killing them. Films of oil on the ocean's surface may also decrease the ability of water to absorb atmospheric gases, thereby killing aquatic animals and plants.

Oil spills can also cause serious economic damage when organisms are not actually killed. Hydrocarbons with foul tastes and smells may be ingested by lobsters, crabs, and other commercially valuable aquatic organisms. Even if the organisms are not killed or injured, they may acquire a taste or odor that makes them unsuitable for human consumption.

Interestingly, the environment may even be damaged by one of the methods used for treating oil spills. Detergents are sometimes added to oil spills to emulsify and disperse the oil. However, the detergent-oil mixtures tend to adsorb to the surface of plants and animals more efficiently than oil alone. Thus the detergent treatment may make the oil more toxic than it would be alone.

Controlling Oil Spills

Methods for the control of oil spills fall into one of about five major categories. First, efforts are now being made to build oil tankers that are less likely to lose their cargo in an accident. By the year 2015, all tankers will be required to be double-hulled.

Second, straightforward mechanical methods are often used to skim oil off the surface of water, sweep it from contaminated beaches, rake up clumps of coagulated petroleum, and bulldoze portions of the land on which oil has accumulated. Third, chemicals are used to break down, break apart, or coalesce petroleum, causing it to disperse more quickly or clump together for easier removal.

Fourth, biological agents are now available for the degradation of spilled oil. Scientists have long known that a number of naturally occurring bacteria can metabolize hydrocarbons like those found in crude oil. The products of metabolism are carboxylic acids, carbon dioxide, and water. A typical reaction is shown below.

$$4CH_3CH_2CH_2CH_2CH_3 + 5O_2 \xrightarrow{\text{bacteria}} 4CH_3CH_2CH_2CH_2\underset{\underset{OH}{|}}{C}{=}O + 2H_2O$$

Both natural and bioengineered bacteria are now used for this purpose.

Fifth, scare tactics, such as the use of noise-making devices and floating dummies are used to frighten birds and aquatic organisms away from areas that have been polluted.

EXPLORE   **Exploration Activities**

1. Name the largest single source of petroleum products released to the environment.

2. Explain how oil in the hydrosphere affects plant and animal life.

3. List four methods of dealing with an oil spill.

BACKGROUND

Heavy Metals

A final category of water pollutants includes a number of inorganic materials—such as various metallic elements, salts, **sediments,** and radioactive isotopes—and heat. These pollutants affect water quality in a wide variety of ways.

The term **heavy metal** is used in environmental chemistry to describe a number of elements that are toxic to plants, animals, and/or humans. Table 13 lists some of these elements along with their sources, effects, and suggested limits in drinking water, as established by the U.S. Environmental Protection Agency. Note that because of its important environmental effects, arsenic is included in this section, even though it is a semimetal (metalloid) rather than a metal.

All of these elements occur in nature. At low concentrations, some of them are harmless and may even be beneficial to living organisms. Others may be beneficial to plants and harmful to animals, or vice versa. A few seem to be beneficial at low concentrations but dangerous at higher concentrations.

Heavy metals pose a threat to water, air, and land resources. For example, the combustion of leaded gasoline releases minute particles of elemental lead to the air. That lead may be inhaled by humans and other animals. Once inside the body, the lead may exert toxic effects on the organism. However lead enters the body—through inhalation, in drinking water, or in foods—the biochemical mechanisms by which it causes harmful effects are much the same.

Heavy metals pose a threat to water, air, and land resources.

	HEAVY METAL INFORMATION		
Metal	Major Source(s)	Effect(s)	Drinking Water Standards
arsenic	mining, pesticides, power-generating plants	toxic, carcinogenic (?)	10 ppb
beryllium	power-generating plants	toxic, carcinogenic (?)	4 ppb
cadmium	mining, industrial wastes, water pipes, electroplating plants	kidney damage, hypertension, toxic to aquatic organisms	5 ppb
chromium	electroplating plants	carcinogenic (as Cr^{6+}) (?), essential to human health in trace amounts	100 ppb
copper	electroplating plants; mining, industrial, and municipal wastes	essential to human health in trace amounts; toxic to plants at moderate levels	1.3 ppm
lead	gasoline emissions, industrial wastes, mining, water pipes	anemia, damage to kidneys and nervous system	0
manganese	mining, industrial wastes	toxic to plants in high concentrations	none established
molybdenum	industrial wastes	essential to plants; may be toxic to animals	none established
selenium	agricultural runoff	essential at low levels; toxic and carcinogenic (?) to animals at higher levels	50 ppb

Source: *2002 Edition of the Drinking Water Standards and Health Advisories,* Washington, D.C.: Office of Water, U.S. Environmental Protection Agency, Summer 2002. Available on-line at www.epa.gov/

Table 13

The Biochemistry of Heavy Metal Toxicity

We understand a great deal about the biochemistry of the heavy metals. Scientists have learned that some metals have toxic effects due to their tendency to react with the sulfuydryl (-SH) group in enzyme molecules. Recall that enzymes are proteins. The reaction that occurs between heavy metal and enzyme molecules is shown below.

$$
\begin{array}{c}
H \\
| \\
S \\
| \\
\quad \\
| \\
S \\
| \\
H
\end{array}
\; + \; Pb^{2+} \;\longrightarrow\;
\begin{array}{c}
| \\
S \\
| \\
Pb \\
| \\
S \\
|
\end{array}
\; + \; 2H^{+}
$$

The new S–Pb–S bond between strands denatures the protein molecule, that is, changes its shape so that it can no longer function. As a consequence, the enzyme is deactivated.

A specific example of this reaction is the one between lead ions (Pb^{2+}) and the enzyme that controls the synthesis of hemoglobin. As Pb^{2+} bonds with and deactivates this enzyme, the amount of hemoglobin manufactured by the body is reduced, the production of red blood cells decreases, and anemia develops. The occurrence of anemia is, thus, an early symptom of lead poisoning.

Anemia is only one of many disorders in which lead has been implicated. For example, the element has also been shown to produce nephritis, scar kidney tissue, and damage nerve fibers.

The toxicity of a metal often depends on its chemical state. Elemental mercury, for example, is relatively inert and nontoxic. When swallowed, it has little or no adverse effect on the body. Many people have dental amalgams that contain elemental mercury. Inhaled as a vapor, however, the element is extremely toxic.

> **The occurrence of anemia is an early symptom of lead poisoning.**

The difference between inhalation and ingestion effects seems to be that in the case of inhalation, mercury vapors diffuse out of the lungs and into the bloodstream. From there, mercury is transported rapidly to the brain, where it causes serious damage to the central nervous system.

Similarly, mercury ion (Hg_2^{2+}) is only moderately toxic. It reacts with chlorine ions (Cl^-) in the digestive tract to form insoluble Hg_2Cl_2. In an insoluble form, the ion poses little hazard to the body. In fact, both elemental and univalent mercury have been used for centuries for medical purposes.

Mercuric ion, Hg^{2+}, is an entirely different matter. It is water-soluble, passing easily through the body, into the bloodstream, and into cells. There it reacts with sulfhydryl groups, as illustrated on the previous page, inactivating key enzymes. Although toxic, Hg^{2+} poses a somewhat limited risk to human health. It tends to accumulate in the liver and kidneys, and thus, is excreted relatively quickly.

Perhaps the most toxic forms of mercury are the organometallic forms, monomethyl mercury (CH_3Hg^+) and dimethyl mercury ($(CH_3)_2Hg$). These substances are formed when anaerobic bacteria feeding on lake-bottom sediments convert $HgCl_2$ to one of its organometallic forms.

$$HgCl_2 \xrightarrow{\text{methylcobalamin}} CH_3HgCl + Cl^-$$

$$HgCl_2 \xrightarrow{\text{methylcobalamin}} (CH_3)_2Hg + 2Cl^-$$

The compound that catalyzes these reactions, methylcobalamin, is similar to vitamin B_{12}, cyanocobalamin, and is released by bacteria that produce methane during anaerobic decay.

The danger posed by monomethyl and dimethyl mercury is that both compounds are fat-soluble. When they enter the body, they tend to concentrate and remain in fatty tissue, especially in brain tissue. They are not readily excreted and appear to have a half-life in the body of at least two months. Thus, they have an extended opportunity to produce damage to the central nervous system and other parts of the body.

> **The danger posed by monomethyl and dimethyl mercury is that both compounds are fat-soluble.**

An individual exposed to mercury compounds over an extended period of time, for example, is likely to experience nothing more than mild digestive upset at first. As mercury accumulates, however, the individual experiences progressive anemia, gastric disorders, inflammation and tenderness of the organs, blackening of the teeth, extensive damage to the central nervous system, changes in behavior, renal damage, and eventually death.

This kind of progressive deterioration is characteristic of many forms of heavy-metal poisoning. As a person ingests more of the metal, its concentration in the body increases, and its effects become more severe and more pronounced. Less commonly, the toxic effects of heavy-metal poisoning are immediate and dramatic. Most examples of acute poisoning result from the (usually accidental) massive ingestion of a metal compound by a person or a group of people.

> **Considerable controversy has developed about the proper level of concern we should have about mercury poisoning.**

Considerable controversy has developed about the proper level of concern we should have about mercury poisoning. Prior to 1970, scientists and government officials in the United States were generally not very concerned about the threat of mercury pollution to human health.

That changed in the early 1970s, however, as research studies began to show high levels of mercury in fish taken from American lakes. For a period of time, a state of near-panic developed among some Americans about the dangers of environmental mercury. The EPA quickly adopted the Canadian government's recommended standard of concentrations of no more than 0.5 ppm of mercury in foods. The EPA also imposed severe limitations on the release of mercury by most industries.

Within a short time, questions began to arise about the seriousness of the mercury scare. Studies of preserved fishes showed that mercury levels in U.S. waters probably had changed little in nearly a century. Almost no evidence was found to suggest that human activities had significantly increased the risk posed by mercury in the environment.

The EPA currently has a Maximum Contaminant Level (MCL) of 2 ppm for mercury in drinking water. The MCL is the safest drinking water standard that the EPA can set and that can realistically be met by current water purification methods.

Controlling Heavy-Metal Pollution

Reducing the concentration of heavy metals in the environment is usually an element-by-element problem. By far the most important source of lead in recent decades has been leaded gasoline. At one time, tetraethyl lead [$(C_2H_5)Pb$] was widely used to improve gasoline efficiency. Much of the lead in this additive escapes into the environment, however, when gasoline is burned. By 1968, more than 98% of all atmospheric lead came from this source.

The solution to the lead problem has been, therefore, relatively straightforward: Eliminate the use of tetraethyl lead in gasoline. Since 1975, when restrictions on this gasoline additive went into effect, lead emissions from motor vehicles have been reduced by more than 90%.

Other uses of lead present other problems. For example, at one time, lead compounds were used in paints. The pigment known as "chrome yellow" was made of lead chromate, $PbCrO_4$, and red lead was made of the mixed oxide of lead, Pb_3O_4. White lead, $Pb(OH)_2 \cdot 2PbCO_3$, was the most popular ingredient for interior and exterior white paints.

More than 50 years ago, however, scientists recognized the environmental hazard posed by lead paints. Small children often ate flakes of old paint, accumulating lead in their bodies and developing symptoms of lead toxicity. This toxicity often manifested in stunted physical and mental development.

In response to this threat, the use of lead compounds in interior paints was banned in 1940 and in exterior paints in 1958. Still, many older buildings are covered with lead-based paints, posing a continued threat to children who live in and play around such buildings. Even decades after the ban on lead-based paints, eliminating the hazard of lead poisoning from these sources has been extremely difficult.

Controlling the concentration of other heavy metals has presented a variety of challenges. For example, nearly 1.5 million kilograms of mercury escape into the environment annually during the manufacture of electric equipment, chlorine, paper, paints, and pharmaceuticals. Agriculture, dentistry, and chemical research are also major sources of waste mercury. In the case of this metal,

> **More than 50 years ago scientists recognized the environmental hazard posed by lead paints.**

distinct techniques must be developed by each industry to reduce the amount of mercury it releases into the environment.

Increasing attention has been paid in the past few years to the control of heavy-metal pollutants in domestic and industrial wastes. Some of the techniques that have been developed for removing heavy-metal ions from such wastes are as follows.

- *Precipitation:* Addition of hydroxide or sulfide ion may precipitate a heavy-metal ion, removing it from solution and eliminating it as a toxic hazard. For example:

$$Pb^{2+}(aq) + 2OH^-(aq) \rightarrow Pb(OH)_2(s)$$

$$Cd^{2+}(aq) + S^-(aq) \rightarrow CdS(s)$$

- *Complexation:* Toxic heavy-metal ions can be tied up in complexes, rendering them less dangerous. Ethylenediaminetetraacetic acid (EDTA) is commonly used for this purpose. The formula below shows how a heavy metal is complexed by EDTA.

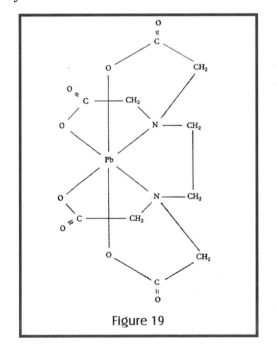

Figure 19

Either precipitation or complexation can also be used to immobilize toxic ions that have been ingested. For example, a child who has eaten paint chips containing lead may be given EDTA. The EDTA forms complexes with the lead and prevents it from exerting toxic effects in cells.

> **Toxic metal ions can be reduced by more active metals, causing them to precipitate out of water.**

Cementation: Toxic metal ions can be reduced by more active metals, causing them to precipitate out of water and reducing their toxic hazard. For example:

$$Cu^{2+}(aq) + Fe(s) \rightarrow Fe^{2+}(aq) + Cu(s)$$

The above reaction can be commercially viable if scrap iron is used as the source of the reactant iron.

Physical processes: A variety of physical changes can also be used to inactivate toxic metal ions. For example, wastewater can be passed through a carbon filter that removes ions through adsorption. Reverse osmosis and ion exchange are also used for the physical removal of heavy-metal ions.

Exploration Activities

1. Name six elements that are regarded as heavy metals in environmental chemistry.

2. By what chemical mechanism does lead inactivate enzymes?

3. How does the chemical state of mercury affect its toxicity in humans?

4. By what method has the release of lead to the environment been reduced?

🔬 BACKGROUND

Other Metal Pollutants

Metals other than those classified as heavy metals may also contaminate or pollute water supplies. One mechanism by which such metals enter water supplies is through **mobilization.** Mobilization is the process by which a metal tied up in some insoluble form is converted to a soluble form.

For example, aluminum is very common on the earth's surface. It is the third most abundant element and the most abundant metal in the earth's crust. It makes up 8.8% of the lithosphere by weight. Aluminum occurs most commonly in minerals that are insoluble in water. These minerals may contain the oxide (Al_2O_3), the hydrated oxides ($Al_2O_3 \bullet xH_2O$), and the silicates ($Al_2O_3 \bullet SiO_2$).

The presence of acids in soil can transform immobilized aluminum to a soluble form, as in this example:

$$Al_2O_3(s) + 6H^+(aq) \rightarrow 2Al^{3+}(aq) + 3H_2O$$

Many compounds of trivalent aluminum (Al^{3+}) are soluble and can become part of a water resource.

The toxic effects of mobilized aluminum have been studied extensively. Aluminum apparently enters the roots of plants and disrupts normal growth and development. Evidence suggests that aluminum exerts these effects not in the form of the Al^{3+} ion but in the form of the hydrated ion $Al(OH)_2{}^+$.

Some researchers believe that aluminum may also be implicated in the human disorder known as Alzheimer's disease. Alzheimer's is a condition in which older people become progressively more senile until they are eventually unable to care for themselves. Hundreds of thousands of Americans and Canadians suffer from this disorder each year.

Recent studies have found high levels of aluminum in brain tissue of individuals who have died of Alzheimer's disease. This finding leads some medical authorities to hypothesize that aluminum may have some role in the development of the disease. The amount of aluminum ingested from water is very low, however, probably no more than 1/20 of that ingested in food. The extent to which

> **Aluminum apparently enters the roots of plants and disrupts normal growth and development.**

> **While not very toxic to most animals, copper may cause damage to plants and algae.**

waterborne aluminum may be a health threat to humans is still, therefore, uncertain.

Mobilization of metal ions may also occur when acidified water passes through water distribution systems. For example, such systems commonly include copper piping. Copper is insoluble in water whose pH is close to 7.0. At lower pHs, however, some copper may dissolve, forming toxic Cu^{2+} ions. While not very toxic to most animals, copper may cause damage to plants and algae.

EXPLORE **Exploration Activities**

1. Describe the mechanism of mobilization.

2. What are the toxic effects of mobilized aluminum?

3. Explain how the mobilization of metal ions can occur in a water distribution system.

BACKGROUND

Sedimentation

When rainwater runs off the land, it usually carries soil with it on its way to a river or lake. The faster the water moves, the larger the particles and the more soil it can carry away. When running water comes to rest, as in a lake, pond, or the ocean, the solid materials held in suspension are deposited. These deposits are sediments.

In this chapter, the term *sediments* is reserved for the insoluble materials carried away by erosion or formed in bodies of water. Recall that a great variety of other materials—phosphates, nitrates, pesticides, and herbicides, for example—may also be washed off the land into lakes and rivers.

Erosion and sedimentation are completely natural phenomena. In fact, many important topographic structures—the Nile and Mississippi River deltas, for example—are evidence of that. Yet, human activities can dramatically increase the rate of erosion and sedimentation.

Soil is typically washed off cultivated land five to 10 times as fast as it is off noncultivated land, 100 times as fast off land on which construction is taking place, and more than 500 times as fast on mined land.

Erosion presents serious land-use problems. In the first decade of the twenty-first century, an average of 3 billion metric tons of valuable topsoil was being lost from farmlands in the United States each year. The impact of such losses on food production is apparent.

But erosion also leads to problems of water pollution. In the first place, finely divided sediments that remain in suspension may reduce the amount of light that reaches aquatic plants, reducing their viability. Also, deposition of suspended sediments can lead to clogged waterways, reducing their usefulness for transportation and recreation. Those sediments can also choke aquatic plants, shellfish, and other aquatic organisms. Finally, suspended sediments must be removed before water can be used for commercial, industrial, and domestic purposes.

> **Human activities can dramatically increase the rate of erosion and sedimentation.**

Sediments can also form as the result of chemical reactions in water. One such reaction occurs naturally when calcium ions in water react with dissolved carbon dioxide.

$$CO_2(aq) + H_2O \rightleftarrows H^+(aq) + HCO_3^-(aq)$$

and

$$Ca^{2+}(aq) + 2HCO_3^-(aq) \rightleftarrows CaCO_3(s) + CO_2(aq) + H_2O$$

These reactions illustrate the important role that oceans play as a sink for CO_2 in the atmosphere.

The metabolic actions of aerobic and anaerobic bacteria in water can also produce sediments. For example, some aquatic bacteria obtain energy from the conversion of the iron(II) ion to the iron(III) ion:

$$4Fe^{2+}(aq) + 4H^+(aq) + O_2(g) \rightarrow 4Fe^{3+} + 2H_2O$$

The iron(III) ion then reacts with water to form insoluble iron(III) hydroxide:

$$Fe^{3+}(aq) + 3H_2O \rightarrow Fe(OH)_3(s) + 3H^+(aq)$$

The presence of iron compounds in a body of water may influence the rate of eutrophication in that body. Apparently, phosphate ion adsorbs on iron(III) hydroxide, removing phosphorus from the aquatic environment and slowing the process of eutrophication. Since the product of a chemical reaction between iron(III) hydroxide and phosphate has not been found in lake sediments, this mechanism seems to involve purely the physical process of adsorption.

Finally, human activities may result in increased sedimentation in lakes and the oceans. Phosphate from wastewater may react with Ca^{2+} ions in water to form the mineral hydroxyapatite:

$$5Ca^{2+}(aq) + OH^-(aq) + 3PO_4^{3-}(aq) \rightarrow Ca_5OH(PO_4)_3(s)$$

EXPLORE   **Exploration Activities**

1. Describe the relative amount of erosion resulting from rainfall on:

    a. uncultivated land

    b. cultivated land

    c. land on which construction is occurring

    d. mined land

2. Write two chemical equations that illustrate processes by which sediments are formed in water.

3. List three ways in which sediments affect aquatic life.

BACKGROUND

Salinity

All naturally occurring water contains some amount of dissolved salts. As streams flow over the ground, they dissolve minerals. These dissolved minerals end up first in lakes and ponds, and eventually in the oceans. The most common ions found in natural waters are Na^+, K^+, Ca^{2+}, Mg^{2+}, Cl^-, CO_3^{2-}, and SO_4^{2-}.

The salinity of freshwater lakes ranges from about 150 mg TDS/L (milligrams of total dissolved solids per liter) to about 4,000 mg TDS/L. In comparison, the salinity of ocean water ranges from 18,000 to 35,000 mg TDS/L. (The unit mg TDS/L is comparable to ppm, or parts per million.)

In most lakes and ponds, fresh water from rivers and streams replaces water lost by evaporation, and salinity remains about constant. In some lakes, water evaporates faster than it is replaced, and salinity constantly increases. For most of this century, the Great Salt Lake in Utah has been an example of this pattern. Until the last decade, it was receiving very little inflow from rivers and streams, and its salinity was continually increasing. Similarly, the salinity of the oceans increases over time, unless global warming causes large-scale melting of polar ice.

Many types of human activity increase the concentration of salts in water. In northern states, for example, salts are used to remove ice from roads during the winter season. These salts eventually wash off roads and into the hydrosphere. Water used by industries usually returns to its source with a higher concentration of salts.

Agricultural operations also increase salinity. Irrigation water dissolves not only naturally occurring minerals in the ground it passes over, but also fertilizers, pesticides, herbicides, and other chemicals used in farming. In some areas, the concentration of salts in used irrigation water has become so high that the water has to be impounded to prevent its further use by humans. In such cases, aquatic organisms using impounded ponds have been killed or badly injured by the high salinity of the water.

> **In most lakes and ponds, fresh water from rivers and streams replaces water lost by evaporation, and salinity remains about constant.**

> **High domestic demand for fresh water can also increase salinity.**

High domestic demand for fresh water can also increase salinity. In California, people in the more populous southern part of the state get much of their water from the wetter northern part of the state. As communities in the Los Angeles area draw more and more water from northern California's lakes and rivers, however, the Pacific Ocean begins to move inland, replacing the fresh waters withdrawn for southern California. Some western lakes and rivers that were once completely filled with fresh water now have a dangerously high salt content as a result of this volume of water use.

Increased salinity presents a problem for all forms of aquatic life as well as for humans. Freshwater plants and animals find it difficult or impossible to adjust to increased salinity in water. Some dissolved salts also present a threat to human health. Elevated levels of Na^+ ion, for example (as from salting of roads), increase health risks for people with hypertension and heart disease. Salts of the heavy metals also present dangers as described in the section on heavy metals.

Exploration Activities

1. How does the salinity of seawater compare with that of freshwater lakes?

2. How does salinity remain constant in most lakes and ponds?

3. What types of human activity increase the salinity of bodies of water?

144

BACKGROUND

Heat

A somewhat different type of pollutant in many areas is warm water. Industries use huge amounts of water for cooling purposes. Plants that generate electrical power from nuclear reactors or fossil fuel combustion are by far the largest consumers of water for cooling.

Such plants withdraw cool water from a nearby river or lake, cycle the water through the plant, and then return the water to the river or lake, generally at an elevated temperature. By one estimate, half of all the water used in the United States is cycled through electric power generating plants. The overall increase in temperature of a lake or river from used water is usually not very great. But increases in the immediate area of the outflow can be significant. The elevation of water temperature as a result of anthropogenic activities is commonly known as **thermal pollution.**

> In general, increasing the temperature of water creates hazards for aquatic life.

In general, increasing the temperature of water creates hazards for aquatic life. In the first place, as water temperature increases, the solubility of oxygen and other gases decreases. At the same time, an increase in temperature causes an increase in metabolic rate, increasing the demand for oxygen. Thus, the survival of fish and other aerobic organisms is threatened.

Also, most aquatic organisms are adapted for life within a relatively narrow temperature range. When water temperatures exceed those ranges, organisms tend to die off. The particular comfort range differs for each organism. Game fish such as trout and salmon are especially sensitive to warm water. Heated water also affects the migration and spawning patterns of most fish.

On the other hand, other aquatic organisms do well in warm water. For slimes, algae, tropical fish, reptiles, and mammals, thermal pollution is an advantage. The large increase in the alligator population in Florida in recent decades is thought to be at least partially the result of increased water temperatures in many parts of the state.

> **One problem in dealing with thermal pollution is that the current method of plant cooling is very inexpensive.**

One problem in dealing with thermal pollution is that the current method of plant cooling is very inexpensive. Alternative methods are much more expensive. One option, for example, is to construct huge cooling towers through which effluent water can be pumped. Evaporation of some of this water reduces the temperature of the remaining wastewater to an acceptable temperature.

Another interesting option makes use of the differential heat sensitivity of various aquatic organisms. The plan is to divert warm wastewater to large cooling ponds filled with organisms that thrive at higher temperatures. These organisms can then be raised and harvested for food. As the water in the pond cools down, it is returned to its original source and replaced with new, warm wastewater.

146

Exploration Activities

1. Why does heated water present a hazard to fish?

2. Describe two alternative methods of plant cooling. Which method is more viable?

BACKGROUND

Introduction

Many communities around the world today are facing an environmental problem new to human societies: an abundance of goods. Throughout most of history, the volume of solid waste that communities produced was relatively small. Since life was technologically simple, household objects were built to last for generations, and discarded materials decayed quickly. People did not have to worry about the amount of wastes they discarded.

All that has changed. Today, communities in most developed countries of the world are generating huge quantities of waste materials—glass bottles, plastic wrappings, metallic tools, and food wastes, for example—much of which will not decay for hundreds or thousands of years. In the United States, at the beginning of the twenty-first century, communities were producing 207 million metric tons of municipal wastes annually, an average of 2.1 kilograms per person per day. In addition, industry was generating another 6.8 billion metric tons of solid wastes each year.

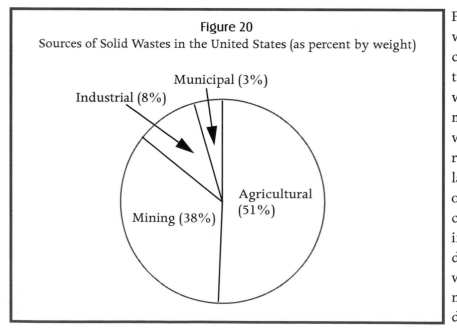

Figure 20
Sources of Solid Wastes in the United States (as percent by weight)

Municipal (3%)
Industrial (8%)
Mining (38%)
Agricultural (51%)

Figure 20 shows where solid wastes in the United States come from. Notice that by far the largest sources of solid waste are agricultural and mining operations. These wastes often accumulate on relatively remote, unoccupied land, with little direct effect on human populations. By comparison, domestic and industrial wastes are usually discarded in urban areas, where they affect much larger numbers of people in more direct ways.

 **Exploration Activities**

1. Name the two largest sources of solid wastes in the United States.

2. Why are the two sources mentioned in the first question usually not regarded as the two most serious problems in terms of generating solid wastes?

BACKGROUND

> **Whatever their source, solid wastes may pose environmental problems for two reasons: their volume and their toxicity.**

Wastes From Mining Operations

Whatever their source, solid wastes may pose environmental problems for two reasons: their volume and their toxicity. The volume of wastes generated by mining operations in the United States is truly staggering. Each year, these operations produce about 1.5 billion metric tons of wastes. That is the equivalent of 5.3 metric tons for each man, woman, and child in the country. Coal mining accounts for about 95% of all U.S. mine wastes.

These wastes are usually left in place, where they were deposited during the mining process. Since they consist primarily of rocks, stones, and gravel, they tend to prevent the growth of new vegetation wherever they are deposited.

Debates about the environmental damage caused by mine wastes have been going on for decades. Objections have been raised about the loss of productive land to mining and the aesthetic damage caused by waste accumulations. As a result of both state and federal legislation, mining companies are now required to restore land they use for mining, returning it to a state at least as good as it was before mining. These laws have not been entirely successful, since some companies prefer to pay the sometimes modest fines they are charged for violating the laws rather than pay the cost of restoring the damaged land.

The processing of ores is another source of solid waste. In mining for metals, the metal itself may actually constitute no more than a few percent of the materials taken from the ground. Removal of the ore from the mixed rock may, therefore, result in a huge volume of residue, known as **tailings.** Again, tailings are often dumped at the site where they are produced.

As with all forms of solid wastes, the volume of mining wastes produced is only part of the problem. Mining wastes are also a matter of concern because of the hazardous chemicals those wastes may contain. The term **hazardous waste** has been defined technically by the U.S. Environmental Protection Agency to include any substance that is flammable, corrosive, reactive, or toxic. The greatest concern about hazardous wastes usually centers

Wastes from mining operations contain a variety of toxic chemicals that may be leached out by rainwater.

on the final category of this definition, wastes that are toxic to plants, animals, and humans.

Wastes from mining operations, for example, contain a variety of toxic chemicals that may be leached out by rainwater. Small concentrations of lead, zinc, arsenic, and other toxic elements may seep into nearby rivers and lakes or may be blown away by winds.

Probably the most serious leaching problem is the conversion of sulfides in mine wastes and tailings to sulfuric acid. The equation below represents a typical reaction by which sulfuric acid is formed in mine wastes.

$$4FeS_2 + 15O_2 + 14H_2O \rightarrow 4Fe(OH)_3 + 8H_2SO_4$$

The presence of both toxic metals and sulfuric acid in streams and lakes is a severe environmental hazard to organisms that live there. In some regions where mining is done, streams and rivers are considered dead, that is, all organisms in them have been destroyed by runoff from mine wastes and/or tailings. By one estimate, 16,000 km of waterways in the Appalachian Mountains have been seriously polluted by runoff from mining activities.

Exploration Activities

1. Why haven't laws requiring mining companies to restore damaged land been more successful?

2. How does the U.S. Environmental Protection Agency define a hazardous waste?

3. Write an equation representing a reaction by which sulfuric acid is formed in mine wastes.

BACKGROUND

Wastes are produced in every farming, ranching, and dairying activity.

Agricultural Wastes

An even larger volume of solid wastes is generated by agricultural activities. Wastes are produced in every farming, ranching, and dairying activity. For example, each dairy bull generates an average of 4 kg of solid wastes per day; each dairy cow, 4.5 kg of wastes; and each head of beef cattle, 1 kg per day. Overall, the latest estimate is that all forms of livestock generate about 1.2 billion metric tons of solid wastes and about a third that amount of liquid wastes every year.

A similar story can be told for farm crops. One researcher has estimated that the production of 1 kg of food leaves behind between 2 and 5 kg of solid wastes in the field and at the factory. As just one example, roughly half of a citrus crop ends up as solid waste in the grove or at the processing plant.

Contributing to this problem is the fact that agricultural operations tend to be concentrated in relatively small areas. At one time, for example, beef cattle normally roamed over acres of land, feeding themselves on range grasses. Today, cattle, chickens, and other livestock tend to be penned into very small areas, such as feedlots. A feedlot is an area where food is brought to animals, in contrast with the traditional practice of having animals forage for their own food.

Feedlots are an economically attractive way of maintaining farm animals. However, they are ecologically questionable because animal wastes are concentrated in a much smaller area than the waste of free-ranging animals.

Manure and plant wastes tend to be aesthetically offensive. They look and smell bad. But they also pose a hazard to the health of humans and other animals. They provide an ideal breeding ground for pathogenic organisms. These organisms may be blown away by the wind or washed out of waste piles by rain. In either case, they may be transmitted to humans or other animals.

Pesticide, herbicide, and fertilizer residues may also contaminate the waste pile and, under similar conditions, be carried away into the environment.

> **Certain types of wastes can be used in the manufacture of alternative fuels.**

A number of methods are available for dealing with agricultural waste. Some plant wastes, for example, can be collected and burned. The heat from this process can sometimes be used in homes and factories. Certain types of wastes can also be used in the manufacture of alternative fuels.

The use of animal wastes to make fertilizer seems like an attractive option. Manure is rich in the nutrients needed by most crops. Unfortunately, the places where such fertilizers would be in greatest demand are often far removed from the feedlots where they are produced. Thus, this method for dealing with agricultural solid wastes is not economically viable in most locations.

 **EXPLORE** **Exploration Activities**

1. How do manure and plant wastes pose a hazard to the health of humans and other animals?

2. What factor makes it difficult to utilize animal wastes for fertilizer?

BACKGROUND

Municipal and Industrial Sources

The solid wastes produced by communities consist primarily of paper, glass, metal, plastic, food, and yard materials. Notice in Table 14 that the greatest increase in solid wastes over approximately 40 years has been in the volume of plastics produced. This trend is troublesome, since plastics are the only major category of solid wastes that are not natural products and, thus, are least likely to be biodegradable.

CHANGES IN VOLUME OF SOLID WASTES PRODUCED, 1960–1999
(by percentage of net discards)

Type of Waste	1960	1970	1980	1990	1999
paper	34.0	36.6	36.4	35.4	38.1
glass	7.6	10.5	10.0	6.4	5.5
metals	12.3	11.4	10.2	8.1	7.8
plastics	0.4	2.4	4.5	8.3	10.5
rubber and leather	2.1	2.6	2.8	2.8	2.7
textiles	2.0	1.7	1.7	2.8	3.9
wood	3.4	3.1	4.6	6.0	5.3
food wastes	13.8	10.6	8.6	10.1	10.9
yard trimmings	22.7	19.2	18.1	17.1	12.1
other	1.7	2.1	3.2	3.0	3.2

Source: Materials Generated in the Municipal Waste Stream, 1960 to 1999, on-line at www.smallbiz-enviroweb.org

Table 14

Most industries produce significant quantities of solid wastes. These wastes consist of a very wide variety of materials, from plant and animal wastes produced during food processing to hazardous chemicals released as by-products of chemical manufacturing to hydrocarbons and petroleum by-products produced during the refining and transportation of petroleum.

The largest volume of industrial wastes is generated by the chemical, primary-metal, paper, and food-processing industries. However, the volume of wastes generated is not necessarily the most important factor in considering industrial waste production. Although the petroleum and electronic industries tend to generate relatively small amounts of solid wastes, compared to other industries, those wastes are significantly more likely to include hazardous materials that pose a threat to the health of humans and other animals.

The problems posed by municipal and industrial wastes are somewhat different from those posed by mining and agricultural wastes. Overall, the total volume of wastes from municipal and industrial sources is much less than that from mining and agricultural sources. However, municipal and industrial wastes tend to be concentrated in areas that are heavily populated.

Traditionally, communities and industries have disposed of their wastes in one of two ways: by disposing of them in landfills or dumping them into the oceans, lakes, or other bodies of water. The use of landfills is becoming more difficult because in many areas, there is simply no space left to dump municipal and industrial wastes. In fact, some cities now find it necessary to ship their wastes dozens or hundreds of miles away to less populated regions for disposal.

In 2001, for example, New York City closed its last landfill, the Fresh Kills landfill on Staten Island. At that point, the city was forced to ship its municipal wastes to other locations in New Jersey, Pennsylvania, Ohio, Georgia, and South Dakota. This long-range shipping of wastes raised the cost of waste disposal for New York citizens from about $42 per ton to $70–$100 per ton. With urban land a highly valuable commodity, dump sites are an increasingly questionable way of using that land.

Dumping wastes into the oceans and other bodies of water has now largely been discontinued, primarily as the result of a series of laws passed by federal, state, and local governments. More and more governmental entities and industries are being faced with the question of how they will dispose of the huge quantities of wastes produced each year.

> **In many areas, there is simply no space left to dump municipal and industrial wastes.**

157

Environmental Hazards of Municipal and Industrial Wastes

Domestic and industrial wastes also pose an environmental risk because of the hazardous materials they may contain. Each industry produces its own type of hazardous waste. The leather industry, for example, must dispose of chromium and iron compounds, sulfuric acid, a variety of organic compounds, and oxides of phosphorus. Textile mills release sulfuric acid, sodium hydroxide, chlorine, salts of iron and tin, and toxic organic compounds. Chemical plants are the source of an almost endless variety of hazardous materials, including chlorine; hydrochloric, hydrocyanic, and sulfuric acids; compounds of arsenic, lead, and mercury; and many toxic organic compounds, such as benzene, toluene, carbon disulfide, carbon tetrachloride, phenol, ethylene, and aniline.

> **Chemical plants are the source of an almost endless variety of hazardous materials.**

Private households are also the source of hazardous chemicals. Many common products used around the home are toxic. Among these are pesticides, paints and paint products, motor oil, plastics, batteries, and spoiled foods. The volume of these hazardous chemicals is small compared with what is produced by industry. But industries often have well-planned systems for the disposal of their wastes, while individual homes do not.

Because there is often no simple alternative, people in private homes may simply dump their hazardous wastes down the drain or into the trash can. These hazardous wastes then become part of the community's overall waste disposal problem.

In the great majority of cases, hazardous wastes become a threat to humans when the wastes enter the atmosphere or hydrosphere. As an example, volatile organic substances discarded by industries evaporate quickly and enter the atmosphere. On a worldwide basis, the risk from these substances is very low. However, in local areas, where large volumes of chemical wastes have been dumped, the risk may be substantial.

The more serious risk to human health is the transport of hazardous chemicals into the hydrosphere. Substances in dumps may wash off the earth's surface and get into rivers or lakes. Or they may seep into groundwater and be transported to surface waters. There they may contaminate drinking water or make bodies of water unsuitable for swimming, boating, fishing, or other recreational activities.

The release of hazardous wastes to the hydrosphere usually does not result in an immediate disaster. Newspaper reports seldom carry accounts of sickness and/or deaths among large numbers of people who have consumed polluted water. Instead, these effects are more likely to develop over long periods of time, resulting in diseases like cancer or in the birth of deformed children.

> **Effects are likely to develop over long periods of time, resulting in diseases like cancer or in the birth of deformed children.**

The Case of PCBs

An instructive example involves the group of chemicals known as polychlorinated biphenyls (PCBs). The term refers to a family of compounds produced when chlorine reacts with biphenyl, as shown below.

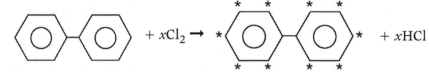

Chlorine may substitute for hydrogen at any one or more of the 10 starred positions in the product. Shown below are three of the more than 200 possible products of this reaction.

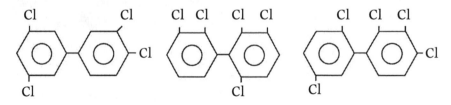

Chlorinated hydrocarbons like those shown here tend to be unreactive. They are soluble in fats but insoluble in water.

First produced in the 1920s, the members of the PCB family have a number of properties that make them highly desirable for industrial uses. For example, they are fire-resistant and very stable. By the 1970s, industry had established numerous uses and applications of PCBs as insulators and cooling fluids and in plastics, adhesives, paints, inks, sealants, pesticides, and specialized papers. They were also used to control dust on roads.

In 1968, however, first reports of PCBs' potential threat to the environment began to appear. Residents of southern Japan accidentally consumed rice oil contaminated with 2,000–3,000 ppm of PCB. These people experienced many medical problems, including swelling of joints, nerve pain, jaundice, abnormal liver function, discharge from the eyes, hearing and visual disturbances, and general weakness. Abnormalities in babies born to women who had eaten the oil were also detected.

> **When articles made from PCBs were discarded, the PCBs soaked into the ground, were carried along by groundwater, and reached rivers, lakes, and the oceans.**

Over the next decade, scientists began to notice increasing levels of PCBs in soil, water, and organisms in many parts of the United States and around the world. The chemicals were apparently escaping during production and use of various products containing the material. Also, when articles made from PCBs were discarded, the PCBs soaked into the ground, were carried along by groundwater, and reached rivers, lakes, and the oceans.

From there PCBs made their way into plants, domestic and wild animals, and eventually humans. Studies of Lake Michigan ecosystems found a biological magnification that began with an initial concentration of 5×10^{-6} ppm in lake water and increased to 5–6 ppm in small fish such as lake herring and alewives, to 10–20 ppm in salmon and lake trout. For comparison, the maximum amount of PCBs recommended for human ingestion by the U.S. Food and Drug Administration is 0.2–3 ppm, and the maximum contaminant level established by the EPA for PCBs in the environment is 0.5 ppm. Thus, consumption of a single lake trout from Lake Michigan would provide a human with five to 10 times the maximum amount recommended by the FDA.

PCBs may also have toxic effects on organisms other than humans. Little information is available on the effect on animals in the wild, although one instance of mink poisoning from the ingestion of PCB-contaminated salmon has been reported. Also, the decline of otter populations in some regions is thought to be due to PCB poisoning.

Laboratory experiments with rats, guinea pigs, pigeons, trout, and other animals have shown that ingestion of PCBs may result in the development of cancers and birth defects.

Confronted with data on the toxic effects of PCBs, the U.S. Congress passed a law banning the manufacture of these compounds after January 1979. Studies conducted since that time indicate that PCB levels in air, water, the ground, and in a variety of organisms are slowly decreasing. For example, PCBs in lake trout taken from the Great Lakes have declined by anywhere from 79% to 92% between 1974 and 2000.

While such figures are encouraging, they do not suggest that the problem of PCB pollution has been solved completely. For one thing, although PCBs are no longer manufactured in the United States (and most other parts of the world), they are still present in many types of equipment throughout the nation. And they sometimes escape into the environment during use or when a piece of equipment is discarded. In 2002, for example, the EPA fined a company called Clean Harbors Inc. for improperly disposing of 180 large capacitors that contained PCBs, allowing their escape into a landfill in upstate New York.

Overall, the EPA has reported an increase in the number of PCB spills reported annually to its offices (from 82 to 302) between 1998 and 2002 and an increase in the number of fish advisories, in which people are advised not to eat PCB-containing fish, from 679 to 764 in the same period.

And humans are still concerned about the effects of PCBs on their health. In 2002, 20,000 current and former residents of Anniston, Alabama, filed suit against the Monsanto Chemical Company because of their exposure to PCBs used by the company at its Anniston plant between 1929 and 1971. Residents argued that they were experiencing unusually high levels of cancer, heart disease, and diabetes as a result of their exposure to Monsanto's PCBs.

> **The EPA has reported an increase in the number of PCB spills reported annually to its offices between 1998 and 2002.**

Other Hazardous Chemicals in Solid Wastes

PCBs are by no means the only chemicals in solid wastes about which there is concern. The EPA has listed hundreds of compounds that are potential threats to the environment and to human health. The Comprehensive Environmental Response, Compensation, and Liability Act of 1980 (CERCLA), commonly known as Superfund, requires the EPA to prepare a priority list of the most hazardous chemicals annually. The top 25 chemicals on the 2001 list are shown in Table 15.

TOP 25 HAZARDOUS SUBSTANCES, 2001
(as determined by the EPA)

Rank	Chemical Name
1	arsenic
2	lead
3	mercury
4	vinyl chloride
5	polychlorinated biphenyls (PCBs)
6	benzene
7	cadmium
8	benzo(αH)pyrene
9	polycyclic aromatic hydrocarbons (PAHs)
10	benzo(βH)fluoranthene
11	chloroform
12	dichlorodiphenyltrichloroethane (DDT)
13	aroclor 1254
14	aroclor 1260
15	trichloroethylene
16	dibenzo(a, h)anthracene
17	dieldrin
18	chromium (hexavalent)
19	chlordane
20	hexachlorobutadiene
21	dichlorodiphenyldichloroethylene
22	coal tar creosote
23	aldrin
24	phosphorus, white
25	benzidine

Source: Agency for Toxic Substances and Disease Registry, "2001 CERCLA Priority List of Hazardous Substances," available on-line at www.atsdr.cdc.gov

Table 15

The hazard posed by each chemical in the list varies widely from place to place. Certain locations are hot spots for one or more substances. That is, these locations have dangerously high concentrations of a particular substance. For example, the concentration of trichloroethylene at one groundwater test site in Pennsylvania was reported to be 27,300 ppb, nearly 300 times the maximum level allowed by the EPA.

Hazards also vary from time to time. Occasionally a plant will release—usually by accident—an abnormally large volume of hazardous waste all at once.

For example, the city of Huntington, West Virginia, has on more than one occasion had to deal with the accidental discharge of carbon tetrachloride into its domestic water supply.

Overall, the nation's public health authorities are most concerned about the long-term health effects of hazardous wastes that have accumulated in dump sites over many years or decades. Deciding how to neutralize the health effects of those waste sites as well as reduce the current volume of toxic chemicals being dumped is a major issue today.

 **EXPLORE**   **Exploration Activities**

1. What chemical property or properties of PCBs make them both a desirable industrial material and a potential environmental hazard?

2. Name five chemicals classified by the EPA as toxic pollutants.

BACKGROUND

Disposal

Solid wastes are disposed of in a variety of ways. Some methods are used primarily for municipal wastes, others primarily for industrial wastes. Probably the method most familiar to the general public is a dump. The term **dump** is rather general, referring to a range of disposal sites. The simplest kind of dump is simply an open area where wastes are deposited. Until the last half century, open dumps were the most popular form of solid waste disposal. Communities simply found an unused space in their vicinity and deposited their wastes there.

Open dumps have become an unsatisfactory method of waste disposal for many reasons. First, as communities grow in size and as people use more disposable materials, dumps simply occupy too much space. Second, volatile wastes from open dumps get into the air and contribute to air pollution. Fires in dumps add to this pollution and also release toxic substances when some materials burn. Most important, toxic wastes leach out of dumps, pass into groundwater, and become part of the hydrosphere.

Attempts to improve the quality of dump sites have led to the development of **sanitary landfills.** A landfill is a disposal site where layers of clean earth are added periodically on top of layers of compacted municipal wastes. Landfills solve many of the problems found in open dumps. Fires are almost impossible, volatile chemicals are less likely to escape to the air, and insects and rodents cannot live in landfills.

An important advantage is that, once filled, the sanitary landfill can eventually be used as a park or an open space, or as land for a housing development.

The major drawback of landfills is that they usually provide no protection against the loss of chemicals to groundwater. In some cases, sites are selected because they lie on relatively impervious materials, such as rock or heavy clay. Still, most communities make no effort actually to seal off the bottom of the landfill, with the result that some wastes still leach out into the soil.

> **Open dumps have become an unsatisfactory method of waste disposal for many reasons.**

Another method of waste disposal is by incineration. Most components of municipal waste are combustible. Plants can be built that will separate combustible from noncombustible wastes and then burn the former. Energy produced in such plants can be used to generate electricity, to heat buildings in the community, or for industrial purposes.

The major disadvantage of waste incineration is the amount of gaseous pollution incinerators may release as a by-product of their operation. The most abundant pollutant released by incinerators is carbon monoxide, followed by SO_2, nitrogen oxides, and hydrocarbons. Recall that these gases are major contributors to air pollution.

Hydrogen chloride is also released during the incineration of solid wastes. A common component of those wastes is polyvinyl chloride (PVC), a plastic used as a rubber substitute in many products, such as shoe soles, tubing, raincoats, gaskets, and upholstery, and as covering for electric wires and cables. When polyvinyl chloride burns, it produces hydrogen chloride, which may then escape from an incinerator into the atmosphere:

$$[-CH_2-CHCl-]_n \rightarrow HCl(g) + \text{other products}$$

Hydrogen chloride dissolves in water droplets in the atmosphere, forming hydrochloric acid. In addition to attacking metal, stone, and other inorganic materials, HCl is an eye and throat irritant.

Incineration of wastes also releases particulates that may contain toxic components such as lead, zinc, and manganese. Many pollution control systems now in use do not capture the kind of fine ash that carries these toxic materials. The ash thus becomes an air pollution problem and, when it settles to the earth, a component of water pollution.

Recent progress in finding methods for the reduction of toxic and harmful pollutants has been encouraging, making incineration an increasingly attractive waste disposal option.

Conservation and Resource Recovery

An approach to the solid waste problem that is becoming more popular is conservation. Efforts are made to reduce the volume of solid wastes produced and to recover from solid wastes materials

> **Incineration of wastes also releases particulates that may contain toxic components such as lead, zinc, and manganese.**

that can be reused. One example of the former is the effort of some supermarkets to get customers to reuse their paper grocery bags. Until recently, each grocery bag was normally used once, then thrown out or used for garbage. Now, some stores pay customers a small premium, such as 5¢, for each bag they return and reuse. This is one way of reducing the amount of paper waste discarded.

> **Recycling of some materials has been going on for decades.**

Recycling is a program for separating wastes into various categories and then selecting those materials that can be removed, reprocessed, and reused. Recycling of some materials has been going on for decades. For example, American industries recycled 58.4% of all steel cans, 84.1% of all the steel found in appliances, and 95% of the steel used in cars in 2000. In addition, larger structures, such as machinery, girders, concrete reinforcement, and other steel materials are routinely recovered, melted down, and used again in new products.

More recently, attention has been given to the recovery of materials that were once simply thrown away and forgotten: paper, glass, and aluminum, for example. Sometimes the recycling process is fairly direct. Glass bottles, for example, can be melted down and recast as new glass bottles. Paper can be reduced to pulp and reused in new paper products.

In other cases, a material can be recovered for use in a new form. For example, used glass can be crushed and made into bricks or road-paving material. Waste paper can be converted into a synthetic form of petroleum.

An important consideration in recycling is economics. If materials are abundant and inexpensive, and if dump sites are plentiful and safe, there will be little incentive for recycling. But as resources become scarce and expensive, and as dump sites become less available and hazardous, resource recovery will seem more attractive to a community.

Recovery of some materials presents difficult technological problems. For example, the volume of plastics discarded is increasing each year. Waste plastics are becoming an increasingly serious municipal waste problem. But many different kinds of plastics are used in commercial products. Each plastic has its own set of chemical and physical properties, which makes separation and recycling difficult.

166

On the most general level, for example, thermoplastic plastics have to be separated from thermosetting plastics. The former can be reheated, reshaped or remolded, and reused. The polyethylene used in packaging materials, toys, and electrical insulation is an example of a thermoplastic plastic.

Thermosetting plastics, in contrast, are destroyed by reheating. The Melmac used in some types of plastic dishes is an example of a thermosetting plastic.

Furthermore, many types of plastic decompose to produce toxic gases when heated. Recall the example of polyvinyl chloride incineration. Physical and chemical processes used in recycling such plastics will release toxic gases to the atmosphere.

Industrial Wastes

Industrial solid wastes tend to pose a unique problem distinct from the challenges posed by municipal solid waste disposal. That problem is the likelihood of hazardous chemicals being present in wastes. A city's wastes are likely to contain large amounts of decayed and decaying food; lawn clippings; wood, glass, plastic, rubber, and other common materials, but few substances that are likely to pose a threat to human health. By contrast, hazardous chemicals, like those listed in Table 15, are commonly found in industrial wastes.

In spite of the dangers posed by industrial wastes, the vast majority of plants and factories have routinely disposed of their wastes in dumps or landfills. Hazardous materials present in those wastes then tend to leak into the surrounding earth, escape into the groundwater, or evaporate into the air.

In 1980, the U.S. Congress created the most extensive program ever developed for the control of industrial wastes. That program was created in the Comprehensive Environmental Response, Compensation, and Liability Act of 1980 (CERCLA). CERCLA created a trust fund of $1.6 billion for the purpose of locating, investigating, and cleaning up the most contaminated disposal sites in the nation. Superfund was envisioned to be a cooperative effort of the federal, state, and local governments working in coordination with industries responsible for such disposal sites. As of 2003, Superfund has been responsible for the assessment of 44,418 sites,

> **In spite of the dangers posed by industrial wastes, the majority of plants and factories have disposed of their wastes in dumps or landfills.**

of which 33,106 (75%) have been removed from the list of hazardous sites. The remaining 11,312 sites remain on the program's site assessment program or have been transferred to the National Priorities List of sites that require cleanup.

For much of its history, the Superfund program has been the subject of considerable controversy among business leaders, government officials, and politicians. Some public officials believe that asking industry to pay for cleanups of its own waste facilities is an unfair intrusion on business, and that governmental agencies should assume responsibility for such actions. Other public officials argue that waste production is a normal and natural part of the industrial process, and that companies should be allowed to deal with this part of their business in whatever way they best can. Still other officials argue that Superfund does not go far enough, and that the amount of hazardous waste in the United States is so large that an even more ambitious program of cleanup is necessary.

Industrial Waste Disposal Systems

In spite of leakage problems, sanitary landfills are still the most popular method of waste disposal. The most conscientious companies use only **secure landfills,** landfills lined with impervious materials to prevent the escape of wastes. By some estimates, however, secure landfills constitute no more than 5% of all waste disposal systems used by industries. In contrast, unsafe methods of dumping and incineration are used for at least 90% of all industrial wastes generated in the United States today.

Chemists can play an important role in dealing with hazardous wastes. The problems to be solved differ from site to site, but a few chemical processes are widely applied. These include neutralization, oxidation-reduction reactions, and precipitation.

- *Neutralization:* Wastes may be very acidic or very alkaline, requiring treatment that will neutralize either H^+ or OR^-. These are typical reactions:

$$2H^+(aq) + Ca(OH)_2(s) \rightarrow Ca^{2+}(aq) + 2H_2O$$

or

$$2OH^-(aq) + H_2SO_4(aq) + 2H_2O + SO_4^{2-}(aq)$$

> **The most conscientious companies use only secure landfills, landfills lined with impervious materials to prevent the escape of wastes.**

168

- *Oxidation or reduction:* A hazardous species can be converted to a less dangerous form by one or the other of these two reactions. For example, toxic cyanide ion can be oxidized with chlorine to a less toxic form, cyanate:

$$2CN^-(aq) + Cl_2(g) + 2OH^-(aq) \rightarrow 2CNO^-(aq) + H_2(g) + 2Cl^-(aq)$$

- *Precipitation:* The hazards of toxic materials can be reduced by converting them from soluble to insoluble forms. For example, this treatment converts toxic chromate ion to insoluble chromium(III) sulfide:

$$8CrO_4^{2-}(aq) + 15S^{2-}(aq) + 20H_2O \rightarrow 4Cr_2S_3(s) + 3SO_4^{2-}(aq) + 40OH^-(aq)$$

> **The advantage of at-sea incineration is that combustion takes place far from any populated areas.**

Hazardous industrial wastes can also be disposed of by incineration. This method is especially effective with organic wastes, since such compounds burn to produce primarily carbon dioxide and water if combustion temperatures are high enough. Incinerators that operate at temperatures of about 1,200°C are often able to destroy 99.99% of all combustible toxic wastes.

Incinerators have sometimes been installed on ships that actually perform the combustion reaction at sea. For example, the Dutch ship *Vulcanus* incinerated large quantities of Agent Orange, a highly toxic herbicide used in the Vietnam War, for the United States government. The advantage of at-sea incineration is that combustion takes place far from any populated areas. Any hazardous gases that are produced and released during the combustion are dispersed with relatively low risk to human populations. Government studies showed, for example, that incineration on the *Vulcanus* produced essentially no measurable hazardous emissions at onshore sites.

Finally, some hazardous wastes are disposed of in deep wells. The petroleum industry has used deep-well injection for more than 150 years to get rid of some of the hazardous wastes it produces. It dumps those wastes back into the wells from which petroleum was originally extracted. Those wells usually end in a permeable zone of rock that is sandwiched between two impermeable layers above and below it. This arrangement may prevent wastes from migrating out of the permeable layer into groundwater. Locations with a favorable geological condition like this can be used for the dispersal of all forms of hazardous wastes.

Experience has shown that even the best storage tanks tend to leak after a certain number of years.

Some objections have been raised to both incineration at sea and deep-well injection. In the former case, some people continue to worry about the release of toxic chemicals to the atmosphere. We have no way of knowing, they say, what the ultimate fate of such chemicals might be.

In the case of deep-well injection, questions arise as to the possible release of toxic chemicals into groundwater. Experience has shown that even the best storage tanks tend to leak after a certain number of years. Thus, it seems almost inevitable that the hazardous wastes stored in deep wells will ultimately find their way back into the environment.

EXPLORE   **Exploration Activities**

1. How does a sanitary landfill differ from an open dump?

2. Compare the advantages and disadvantages of incineration as a solid waste disposal method.

3. Describe three ways in which specific materials can be recycled.

4. Write two chemical equations that illustrate reactions by which the hazardous effects of toxic wastes can be combated.

5. What geologic condition is necessary in order for deep-well injection to be used in the disposal of hazardous wastes?

Additional Activities

Foundations

1. List some specific environmental problems in your community with which chemists might be involved. Then describe the kinds of research in which chemists might become engaged in solving those problems.

2. The diagram of Earth in Figure 1 is not drawn to scale. Find out the approximate dimensions of each region shown on the diagram and then explain why it is not drawn to scale.

3. Make a line graph that shows how Earth's population has changed from the dawn of the modern era (A.C.E.) to the present day. What is the relevance of this graph to the rise of modern pollution problems?

4. People around the world became aware of pollution problems in the twentieth century to some extent because of a few major disasters in which many human lives were lost or the biosphere was badly damaged. Each of the names listed below refers to one of those disasters. Read about any one of the cases listed. Then write a newspaper article or television news report describing the episode.

   • Meuse Valley, Belgium, 1930

   • Donora, Pennsylvania, 1948

   • London, December, 1952

   • Torrey Canyon, 1967

   • Exxon Valdez, 1989

   • Cayuga River, 1969

5. Many people argue that the modern environmental movement in the United States began with an event known as Earth Day 1970. Search the Internet for information about this event and prepare a list of at least five web sites that contain useful information on this topic.

6. What does an environmental chemist do? Search the Internet for an answer to this question. Then write a job description brochure, "So You Want To Be an Environmental Chemist" that outlines the education requirements, employment opportunities, job outlook, expected types of work, probable salaries, and other matters of interest to prospective environmental chemists.

7. Many environmental organizations maintain a web site that describes their activities. Prepare a list of federal, regional, state, and local government agencies concerned with protecting the environment. Prepare a similar list of nongovernmental agencies, such as the National Resources Defense Council, Clean Water Action, and the Alliance for Clean Air.

The Atmosphere

1. (a) One of the most reactive chemical species in the troposphere is the hydroxyl radical (OH). Draw the electronic structure of this radical and tell how it differs from the hydroxide ion (OH^-).

   (b) How does the electronic structure of the hydroxyl radical explain its chemical activity?

   (c) The OH radical often acts as a "hydrogen scavenger," removing a single hydrogen atom from other chemical species. Write a chemical equation that shows the reaction between a hydroxyl radical and methane (CH_4).

2. Draw the electron dot structure of the following ions:

   O^+ O_2^+ NO^+

   What is it about the structures of these ions that makes them so reactive?

3. Sulfur dioxide (SO_2) and nitrous oxide (NO_x) are produced by both natural and anthropogenic sources. List the major sources of each kind for both gases. Then list the approximate amount of each gas produced by each source.

4. Many instruments and techniques are used in studying the atmosphere. Search the Internet for information on any one of the instruments or techniques listed below. Then write a one-page report on your findings.

   a. Weather balloon

   b. Radiosonde

   c. Computer modeling

   d. Rawinsonde

   e. TIROS I

   f. DC8 or ER-2 aircraft

   g. TOMS

   h. Radiometer

5. The U.S. Congress has passed a number of laws dealing with air pollution. Most states have also adopted air pollution legislation. Listed below are five major national laws. Search the Internet to obtain further information on any one of these national laws or any state law chosen by you or assigned by your teacher. Outline the major provisions of this law.

   a. Air Pollution Control Act of 1955

   b. Clean Air Act of 1963

   c. Clean Air Act of 1965

   d. Clean Air Act of 1970

   e. Clean Air Act of 1990

6. Most states maintain web sites that permit access to the state's environmental agencies with detailed information about air quality legislation, standards, data, etc. Access your own state's web site and determine what information is available about air quality on that web site. Prepare a *Guide to Air Quality Information* that would help a citizen find out more about air quality in your state. Make a list of ways in which the state's web site could be improved to make that information more accessible to citizens.

Atmospheric Pollution

1. Each of the chemicals listed below can be used to remove sulfur dioxide from flue gases. Write a chemical equation for the reaction that occurs between sulfur dioxide and each substance listed.

   a. magnesium hydroxide

   b. sodium hydroxide

   c. calcium carbonate

   d. sodium sulfite and water*

   e. oxygen (with a catalyst)

   f. calcium oxide and oxygen*

   *Only one product is formed.

2. The U.S. Environmental Protection Agency provides detailed data on the concentration of various air pollutants in nearly all regions of the United States. Search the Internet to locate that information for your area (state, city, or region). Write a one-

paragraph summary of the information you find, and list a citation for the information.

3. Search the Internet for web sites that have diagrams of catalytic converters. Make your own drawing of a catalytic converter showing how it differs from the one shown on page 42.

4. What are the major sources of carbon monoxide, sulfur dioxide, and nitrogen oxides according to the most recent data available? Make three pie charts (one for each pollutant) that show the fraction of each pollutant that comes from each source.

5. Search the Internet to find out what people and organizations are currently saying about the problems of acid deposition. Is there consensus about the seriousness of the problem? Make two lists, one giving reasons for optimism about the problem, and one giving reasons for pessimism.

6. Write the chemical formula for each of the following hydrocarbons and tell the major natural and anthropogenic source for each compound listed.

   a. ethene

   b. xylene

   c. 1,3-butadiene

   d. methanal

7. Ozone is produced by a number of different reactions in urban air. Write a series of chemical equations that show how ozone can be produced from the carbon monoxide released during incomplete combustion of gasoline. The overall reaction for that process is: $CO + 2O_2 \xrightarrow{h\nu} CO_2 + O_3$
   The first step in the reaction is as follows: $CO + OH\cdot \rightarrow CO_2 + H\cdot$. Recall that some of

the chemical species present in urban air include $OH\cdot$, NO, and NO_2, as well as oxygen and nitrogen.

8. The study of particulates makes use of certain specialized terms. Find and write the definition for each of the following terms:

   a. aerosol

   b. condensation aerosol

   c. dispersion aerosol

   d. viable particulate

   e. soot

   f. fly ash

   g. $PM_{2.5}$

   h. PM_{10}

9. Search the Internet for information on the major sources of hydrocarbons or volatile organic compounds in polluted air in the United States. Then make a pie chart showing the amounts of hydrocarbons or VOCs produced by each of these sources.

10. Particulates are responsible for several serious respiratory disorders. Prepare a one-page report on any one of the following disorders. The report should include the cause, symptoms, and treatments for the disorder.

    a. asbestosis

    b. berylliosis

    c. black lung

    d. chalicosis

    e. siderosis

    f. silicosis

11. Draw a diagram of any one of the following devices used to control the release of particulates to the air.

    a. gravity settling chamber

    b. cyclone collector

    c. baghouse

    d. wet scrubber

    e. electrostatic precipitator

Changes in the Atmosphere

1. Each of the persons and organizations listed below has had an important role in the issue of ozone layer depletion. Write a two-page biography of any one (or pair) of those listed, with special emphasis on the role in the ozone problem.

    a. Thomas Midgley, Jr.

    b. Mario J. Molina and F. Sherwood Rowland

    c. George Dobson

    d. British Antarctic Survey

    e. Friends of the Earth

    f. Ozone Action

2. One of the major problems in dealing with ozone depletion is finding a satisfactory substitute for CFCs in most commercial uses. One possibility is a group of compounds known as the hydrochlorofluorocarbons (HCFCs). Write a brief newspaper article that explains the chemical structure of the HCFCs and their potential advantages and disadvantages as CFC substitutes.

3. What is the current status of the ozone problem? Can it be said to have been solved, or is it getting worse? Search the Internet to obtain information for a two-page article arguing one side or the other (or, if you prefer, some third position).

4. What is the current policy of the U.S. government with regard to the problem of global climate change? Search the web sites of U.S. organizations and agencies, such as the White House, the Environmental Protection Agency, and the National Oceanic and Atmospheric Administration, to find the answer to this question. Write a one-page summary describing what seems to be the government's official policy about global warming. Then write another one-page essay explaining how and why you agree or disagree with that policy.

5. Search the Internet to find nongovernmental organizations with policies about global warming that differ from those of the U.S. government (Activity 4). Write a two-page article that describes the major points of disagreement between governmental and nongovernmental views of the global warming problem.

6. Choose any one of the eight-stage scenario of global warming to research in more detail. Find out what scientific evidence is available about the stage you choose and any disagreements that have been expressed about the likelihood of that stage occurring. Write a two-page opinion piece in which you express your own conclusions about the probability of the stage actually occurring.

Water Sources

1. Many waterborne diseases are caused by pathogens found in polluted water. Select any one of the diseases listed on the next page to research. Write a report on the disease that lists the causative agent, symptoms, treatment, and incidence (where it is

likely to occur and to what extent) of the disease.

a. cryptosporidiosis

b. *Escherichia coli* O157:H7

c. giardiasis

d. hepatitis A

e. schistosmiasis

f. salmonella

g. amebiasis

h. campylobacter enteritis

2. The U.S. Environmental Protection Agency has established drinking water standards for many pollutants. Find out the current standards for the substances listed below. Create a table that lists these substances, current standards, and at least one source from which the subject may be derived.

a. coliform bacteria

b. antimony

c. mercury

d. vanadium

e. aldrin

f. chlordane

g. DDT

h. 2, 4-D

3. You can learn a great deal about water quality without conducting any chemical tests. Visual observations can provide information on the degree and sources of pollution. A useful guide for this purpose is a booklet entitled *Water Quality Indicators Guide: Surface Waters,* originally published by the U.S. Department of Agriculture in 1988. The guide explains how to test a water source for sediment, animal waste,

nutrients, pesticides, and salinity. The pages for nutrients are reproduced at the end of this appendix.

Select a pond, lake, river, or other water source to study. Complete the information at the top of the form. Read the directions indicated with an arrow (→). Then use the sheet to evaluate the amount of nutrient pollution in the water source you have chosen to study.

Try to find a copy of the *Quality Indicators Guide* so that you can carry out other tests in the body of water you have chosen to study.

Water Pollution

1. Survey a variety of detergents available at a local store. Include dry and liquid laundry detergents, solid and liquid dishwashing detergents, and specialized cleaning materials. For each ingredient you find on the labels of these products, find out the ingredient's function and any risk it may present to the environment. Make a chart that shows the function and environmental hazard (if any) of each ingredient you identify.

2. Search the Internet to find out what regulations have been established by the federal government and by your own state government on the use of phosphates, NTA, or other builders in the manufacture of syndets.

3. Thirty years after its ban, DDT continues to be a source of controversy among government officials, scientists, and ordinary citizens. Search the Internet to find arguments for and against its use as a pesticide in the United States and other parts of the world. Prepare a two-page paper that outlines

your own position on the use of DDT as a pesticide in the United States *or* in any other nation you choose.

4. The information most people have about oil pollution in the oceans comes from a few well-known major disasters. For each of the events listed below, describe briefly how the accident occurred and what short- and long-term effects it had on the environment.

   a. *Torrey Canyon* (1967)

   b. Santa Barbara offshore well (1968)

   c. *Amoco Cadiz* (1978)

   d. Ixtoc well (Mexico; 1979)

   e. *Exxon Valdez* (1989)

   f. Usinsk (Kolva River, Russia; 1994)

   g. *Erika* (1999)

   h. *Westchester* (2000)

   i. *Prestige* (Spain 2002)

5. Has the problem of ocean pollution by petroleum products become more or less severe in the last 40 years? Search the Internet for data that will help answer this question. Then make a graph that shows trends in ocean pollution by petroleum products as measured by some variable, such as metric tons of oil spilled per year.

6. Humans and other animals are seldom exposed to large doses of heavy metals all at once. A few terrible disasters are exceptions to that statement. Select any one of the following events to study in detail. Then write a two-page article describing the event, its causes, and its ultimate resolution (if any).

   a. Minamata Bay, Japan, 1953

   b. Morinaga arsenic-milk, 1955

   c. Kanemi, Japan, 1968

   d. Itai Itai, Japan, 1995

   e. Kesterson Reservoir, 1980s and later

   f. Pica among urban poor children (current)

7. Mining operations pose a serious environmental hazard in certain regions. Read enough about these hazards so that you can prepare a brief report on any one of the following topics.

   a. The chemistry of acid mine drainage

   b. Biological and physical effects produced by acid mine drainage

   c. Methods of controlling acid mine drainage

   d. Federal and/or state regulations dealing with acid mine drainage

8. You are the Environmental Control Officer for your local community, charged with monitoring water quality and providing for the installation of systems that will control water pollution. The most significant water pollution problem in your community at the present time is **X**, where **X** may be any one of the problems listed below. What methods are available for the control of **X**? Prepare a two-page memorandum for the city council, county commissioners, or other local governing body that describes a system that will lead to a reduction in any one (your choice) of the problems listed below.

   a. sedimentation

   b. excess salinity

   c. thermal pollution

   d. heavy metal in the water

9. Your local electrical power provider, Central Power, plans to construct a new nuclear power plant on the Snohamish River that runs through your community. The plant will be located 10 km upstream from your community. It will discharge cooling water into the Snohamish at a temperature 2.5°C higher than its intake temperature. Choose any one of the following positions and write a two-page report providing scientific, economic, and other data to support the choice you make.

   a. Plant construction should be prohibited until the temperature of cooling water returned to the river is reduced by X°C. (You decide what X should be.)

   b. Plant construction should be permitted under the existing design.

   c. Plant construction should be permitted under the existing design, provided that the following environmental provisions are added to protect the environment: (You decide what provisions must be added.)

   d. Plant construction should be prohibited, no matter what changes are made to the existing design.

Solid Wastes

1. What federal laws control the disposal of mine wastes? Are there such laws in your state? From a search on-line, choose any one federal or state law dealing with mine wastes (coal or metal). Write a report that lists the major provisions of that law. Then find out to what extent that law has been effective in reducing waste disposal problems from mining. Include in your Internet survey federal and state governmental sites, as well as web pages maintained by environmental groups and industrial associations.

2. What are the specific environmental hazards posed by feedlots? When you have found an answer to this question on the Internet or in reference books, prepare a memorandum for county commissioners of a rural area, outlining specific restrictions that should be placed on the creation and operation of any feedlot.

3. Every community has to find a way to get rid of municipal wastes. What system does your community use? Form a research committee of other class members and have the committee consult with a local waste disposal company. Prepare a report that describes (a) the current system used for waste disposal, (b) any current or anticipated future problems that system may face, and (c) any changes that are planned to deal with those problems.

4. Federal, state, and local governments have passed a number of laws dealing with solid waste disposal. Search the Internet to find some examples of those laws. Then choose any one law to study in more detail. Prepare a report that outlines the main provisions of that law and, to the extent possible, how effective that law has been.

5. The disposal of radioactive wastes presents special problems and challenges. What is the nature of those problems and challenges? You have been asked to write an article for a popular magazine on the subject "Is Yucca Mountain the Answer?" Search the Internet for information on the disposal of radioactive wastes in general and the Yucca Mountain solution in particular. Then write a three- to four-page article that fits the assigned topic.

Nutrients

FIELD SHEET 3A: NUTRIENTS
INDICATORS FOR RECEIVING WATERCOURSES AND WATER BODIES*

Evaluator _____ Date _____

Water Body Evaluated _____ County/State _____

Water Body Location _____ Total Score/Rank _____

(Circle one number among the four choices in each row which BEST describes the conditions of the watercourse or water body being evaluated. If a condition has characteristics of two categories, you can split a score.)

Rating Item	Excellent	Good	Fair	Poor
1. Total amount of aquatic vegetation at low flow or in pooled areas. Includes rooted and floating plants, algae, mosses, and periphyton	• Little vegetation, uncluttered look to stream or pond OR What's expected for good water quality conditions in your region • Usually fairly low amounts of many different kinds of plants • OTHER ___ 10	• Moderate amounts of vegetation OR What's expected for good water quality conditions in your region • OTHER ___ 6	• Cluttered, weedy conditions, vegetation sometimes luxurious and green • Seasonal algal blooms • OTHER ___ 3	• Choked, weedy conditions or heavy algal blooms, or no vegetation at all • Dense masses of slimy white, grayish-green, rusty brown or black water molds common on bottom • OTHER ___ 0
2. Color of water due to plants at base or low flow	• Clear or slightly greenish water in pond or along the whole reach of stream • OTHER ___ 9	• Fairly clear, slightly greenish • OTHER ___ 6	• Greenish, difficult to get pond sample without pieces of algae or weeds in it • OTHER ___ 3	• Very, very green pond scums • Pea-green color or pea soup condition during seasonal blooms of microscopic algae in ponds • Oil-like sheen when pea soup algae die off • OTHER ___ 0
3. Fish behavior in hot weather fish kills, especially before dawn	• No fish piping or aberrant behavior • No fish kills • OTHER ___ 9	• In hot climates, occasional fish piping or gulping for air in ponds just before dawn • No fish kills in last two years • OTHER ___ 5	• Fish piping common just before dawn • Occasional fish kills • OTHER ___ 3	• Pronounced fish piping • Pond fish kills common • Frequent stream fish kills during spring thaw • Very tolerant species (e.g., bullhead, catfish) • OTHER ___ 0

(continued)

	OTHER 8	OTHER 7	OTHER 4	OTHER 2
4. Water use impacts; health effects for whole sub-watershed	• None	• Minimal, such as reduced quality of fishing	A couple of the following: • Algal-clogged pipes • Algal-related taste, color, or odor problems with human or livestock water supply • Cattle abortion • Reduced recreational use due to weedy conditions, decay, odors, etc.	Several of the following: • Algal-clogged pipes • Algal-related taste, color, or odor problems with human or livestock water supply • Cattle abortion • Reduced quality of fishery • Reduced recreational use due to weedy conditions, decay, odors, etc. • Blue babies—incidence of methemoglobinemia due to high nitrat levels • Property devaluationo

	OTHER 9	OTHER 7	OTHER 3	OTHER 1
5. Bottom-dwelling aquatic organisms	• Intolerant species occur: mayflies, stoneflies, caddisflies, water penny, riffle beetle • High diversity	• Intolerants common • A mix of tolerants: shrimp, damselflies, dragonflies, black flies • Moderate diversity	• Mainly tolerants: snails, shrimp, damselflies, dragonflies, black flies • Mainly tolerants, but some very tolerants • Intolerants rare • Reduced diversity with occasional upsurges of tolerants; e.g., tube worms and chironomids	• Mainly very tolerants: midges, cranflies, horseflies, rat-tailed maggots or no organisms at all • Very reduced diversity, upsurges of very tolerants common

*The effects of nutrients may be masked by high sediment loads, creating sufficient turbidity to shade light-dependent aquatic vegetation. This may cause aquatic vegetation—a water quality indicator—to die and disappear from the watercourse. To obtain accurate nutrient levels in high-sediment situations, chemical testing may be necessary. Under these circumstances you should contact a local or other water quality specialist.

↑↑ 1. Add the circled Rating Item scores to get a total for the field sheet.

2. Check the ranking for this site based on the total field score. Check "excellent" if the score totals at least 38. Check "good" if the score falls between 23 and 37, etc. Record your total score and rank (excellent, good, etc.) in the upper-right-hand corner of the field sheet. If a Rating Item is "fair" or "poor," complete Field Sheet 3B.

RANKING Excellent (38–45) [   ]   Good (23–37) [   ]   Fair (9–22) [   ]   Poor (8 or less) [   ]

Source: *Water Quality Indicators Guide: Surface Waters,* U.S. Department of Agriculture, Soil Conservation Service (Washington, D.C., 1989), pp. 110–11.

Answer Key

Foundations

Exploration Activities

Environmental Chemistry

1. Environmental chemistry is the study of chemical phenomena in the environment.

2. Some questions environmental chemists try to answer include the following:

   a. What chemical species (elements, compounds, ions, free radicals, etc.) occur in the environment naturally?

   b. Where do these species come from?

   c. How are chemicals transported from one place to another in the environment?

   d. What is the ultimate fate of chemicals in the environment?

   e. What chemical reactions typically occur in the environment?

   f. How do human activities influence chemical species and the reactions that occur among them in the environment?

The Parts of the Earth

1. The four areas into which the earth can be divided are the atmosphere, lithosphere, hydrosphere, and biosphere.

2. The atmosphere is the envelope of gases that surrounds the earth. The lithosphere is made up of rock, soil, and other solid materials. The hydrosphere consists of all of Earth's water resources. The biosphere contains all living organisms on Earth.

Pure Resources

1. Absolutely pure water does not exist naturally on Earth because water dissolves so many different substances so easily.

2. Air is a mixture and water is a compound.

Contaminants and Pollutants

1. A contaminant is any material that is normally not present in some part of the environment but, when present, is harmless to humans and other organisms, while a pollutant is any material present in some part of the environment in greater than normal concentration with the *potential* for causing harmful effects in organisms.

2. Student answers will vary.

Natural Cleansing Processes

1. An anthropogenic pollutant is one produced as the result of human activities.

2. Dilution occurs when a material is distributed throughout the entire volume of the substance into which it is released.

3. A sink is the final location in which a contaminant or pollutant is deposited for an extended period of time.

The History of Pollution

1. Two changes that have increased pollution problems are increases in human populations and developments in modern chemical technology.

2. Pollution often results from technological development and the economic progress it brings, but it often results in a more dangerous environment for humans and other organisms.

Additional Activities

Student answers will vary.

The Atmosphere

Exploration Activities

Structure of the Atmosphere

1. The four layers of the atmosphere are the troposphere, stratosphere, mesosphere, and thermosphere.

2. Ozone is found in the stratosphere. It absorbs UV radiation.

Composition of the Troposphere

1. The most abundant gases produced during the decay of organic matter are methane (CH_4) and nitrous oxide (N_2O). Keeping animals in feedlots also produces these gases.

2. Volcanic action, hot springs, geysers, and sea spray also contribute to the composition of the troposphere.

Anthropogenic Compounds

1. The fossil fuels are coal, oil, and natural gas.

2. Various types of coal differ from one another in the amount of pure carbon, volatile materials, moisture, and sulfur that they contain.

3. Petroleum is refined for the purposes of dividing it into its basic components that can then be used for many different purposes.

Combustion of Fossil Fuels

1. The two most abundant products of the combustion of fossil fuels are water and carbon dioxide.

2. Carbon monoxide and pure carbon are always produced during the incomplete combustion of fossil fuels.

3. The most important anthropogenic source of sulfur dioxide is the combustion of fossil fuels.

4. Oxides of nitrogen are produced during the combustion of fossil fuels, especially petroleum, primarily in motor vehicles.

Types of Pollutants

1. Carbon monoxide; sulfur dioxide and sulfur trioxide; nitrogen oxides; hydrocarbons; photochemical oxidants; particulate matter; other elements and compounds, including ozone, asbestos, heavy metals, ammonia, hydrogen sulfide, sulfuric and nitric acids, and radioactive materials.

2. A primary pollutant is released directly into the atmosphere as the result of human activity. A secondary pollutant is produced in the atmosphere during a chemical reaction or set of reactions among primary pollutants and naturally occurring substances.

Air Quality Standards

1. The Clean Air Act of 1965 focused on problems of air pollution created by motor vehicles—emissions of carbon monoxide and hydrocarbons.

2. Secondary standards are less restrictive than primary standards. Primary standards are designed to protect the health of humans; secondary standards are designed to protect other parts of the environment.

Sources of Pollutants

Anthropogenic pollutants are harmful because they stay in concentrated areas.

Additional Activities

1. a.

$\cdot \overset{\cdot\cdot}{\underset{\cdot\cdot}{O}} \overset{\cdot}{\cdot} H$ $\overset{\cdot\cdot}{\underset{\cdot\cdot}{:O}} \overset{\cdot}{\cdot} H$

  hydroxyl radical   hydroxide ion

The hydroxyl radical has one fewer electron than the hydroxide ion.

b. The hydroxyl radical has a strong tendency to seek an electron to complete its outer octet of electrons.

c. $OH\cdot + CH_4 \rightarrow H_2O + CH_3\cdot$

2. In each case, the species shown is active because it seeks an electron to form an electrically neutral molecule.

$\cdot \overset{\cdot\cdot}{\underset{\cdot}{O}}$ $\overset{\cdot\cdot}{\underset{\cdot\cdot}{O}}:\overset{*}{\underset{**}{*O}}$ $:\overset{\cdot\cdot}{N}\overset{*}{\underset{*}{:O:}}$

3. Students' answers will be obtained from individual research and will vary depending on source and time at which they are obtained.

4.– 6. Student answers will vary.

Atmospheric Pollution

Exploration Activities

Carbon Monoxide

1. Carbon monoxide is added to the atmosphere primarily through the incomplete combustion of organic material. Smaller amounts are added by living green plants that are exposed to sunlight, from dead and decaying plant matter, from the soil and wetlands, from rice paddies, and from bacteria, algae, jellyfish, and other organisms that live in the oceans.

2. $CO(g) + HbO_2(aq) \leftrightarrows HbCO(aq) + O_2(g)$

3. The primary mechanism for controlling carbon-monoxide pollution is to increase the efficiency of internal combustion engines that burn fossil fuels.

4. Reformulated gasoline is gasoline to which some chemical or chemicals, like MTBE or ethanol, have been added to improve the efficiency of combustion of the gasoline.

Nitrogen Oxides

1. As temperature increases, the rate at which NO forms from N_2 and O_2 increases.

2. Various mechanisms have been suggested for the formation of nitrogen acids from nitrogen oxides. Three such mechanisms are the following:

a. $2NO_2 + O_3(g) \rightarrow N_2O_5(g) + O_2(g)$, followed by $N_2O_5(g) + H_2O(l) \rightarrow 2HNO_3(aq)$

b. $HO\cdot + NO(g) + M \rightarrow HNO_3(aq) + M$, where M = some active species

c. $NO_2(g) + O(g) + M \rightarrow NO3(g) + M$ followed by $NO_2(g) + NO_3(g) \rightarrow N_2O_5(g)$ followed by $N_2O_5(g) + H_2O(l)$ $2HNO_3(aq)$.

Sulfur Dioxide

1. Sulfur dioxide is produced by a number of reactions, such as the following:

a. $4FeS_2 + 11O_2(g) \rightarrow 2Fe_2O_3(s) + 8SO_2(g)$

b. S (in organic compounds) $+ O_2(g) \rightarrow SO_2(g)$

c. $2ZnS(s) + 3O_2(g) \rightarrow 2ZnO(s) + 2SO_2(g)$

SO_2 is then converted to sulfuric acid by one of the following reactions:

d. $SO_2 + O_3 \rightarrow SO_3 + O_2$ and $SO_2 + HO\cdot \rightarrow HSO_3\cdot$, followed by $HSO_3\cdot + O_2 \rightarrow HSO_5\cdot$, followed by $HSO_5\cdot + NO \rightarrow HSO_4\cdot + NO_2$, followed by $HSO_4\cdot + NO_2 + H_2O \rightarrow H_2SO_4 + HNO_3$

e. $2SO_2 + 2H_2O + O_2 \xrightarrow{\text{Fe and Mn} \atop \text{salts}} 2H_2SO_4$

2. SO_2 is generally removed by reacting the gas with a basic substance, such as:

$$SO_2(g) + Ca(OH)_2(aq) \rightarrow CaSO_3(aq) + H_2O$$

3. Basic soils tend to counteract the effects of acid deposition more effectively than acidic or neutral soils. One such mechanism is the following:

$$2H^+(aq) + CaCO_3(s) \rightarrow Ca^{2+}(aq) + H_2O + CO_2(g)$$

4. Some effects of acid deposition on the environment include the following:

   a. Acid deposition damages stomata on leaves and destroys root hair. It also leaches minerals from the soil, inhibiting a plant's ability to take up and use nutrients and water.

   b. Acid deposition may cause the death of aquatic organisms.

   c. Acid deposition may cause leaching of toxic minerals from the soil.

Hydrocarbons

1. An aliphatic compound will be any open-chain (acyclic) hydrocarbon, while an aromatic hydrocarbon will be one with a benzene-like structure. A saturated hydrocarbon contains only single carbon-carbon bonds, while an unsaturated hydrocarbon contains at least one double or triple bond.

2. Photochemical oxidants are oxidizing agents produced by light-catalyzed reactions.

3. The reactions by which ozone is produced from NO_2 emissions are the following:

   a. $NO_2(g) \overset{h(\upsilon)}{\rightarrow} NO(g) + O(g)$

   b. $O + O_2 \rightarrow O_3$

4. Industrial smog is formed by a combination of smoke and fog, while photochemical smog is formed by the action of light energy on motor vehicle emissions.

5. Oxidants in photochemical smog attack and destroy enzymes, interrupting vital biochemical processes.

6. The emission of hydrocarbons can be controlled by the use of catalytic converters and by the use of certain physical mechanisms, such as the installation of vapor-control devices on gasoline pumps.

Particulates

1. Natural particulates include bacteria, fog droplets, and pollen, while anthropogenic particulates include fly ash, cement dust, and coal dust. (See Table 9)

2. Particulates block the intercellular spaces in the respiratory system, they may be toxic in and of themselves, and they may carry other toxic materials adhered to their surface.

3. As the centrifuge spins, centrifugal forces throw heavy particles outward, where they can be collected and removed.

4. Electrostatic precipitators operate on the principle that opposite electrical charges attract each other.

Additional Activities

1. a. $Mg(OH)_2 + SO_2 \rightarrow MgSO_3 + H_2O$

    b. $2NaOH + SO_2 \rightarrow Na_2SO_3 + H_2O$

    c. $CaCO_3 + SO_2 \rightarrow CaSO_3 + CO_2$

    d. $Na_2SO_3 + H_2O \rightarrow 2NaHSO_4$

    e. $O_2 + 2SO_2 \rightarrow 2SO_3$

    f. $2CaO + O_2 + 2SO_2 \rightarrow 2CaSO_4$

2.– 5. Student answers will vary.

6. a. Ethene is produced naturally during the ripening and decay of fruits. It is

released from leaky gas lines, in the exhaust from internal combustion engines, and from improperly operating greenhouse heating units.

$$H-\overset{\overset{\displaystyle H}{|}}{C}=\overset{\overset{\displaystyle H}{|}}{C}-H$$

b. Xylene is produced naturally from petroleum sources, during forest fires, and in the emissions given off by plants. It is given off during many operations in which chemical and petroleum products are produced, during the manufacture of certain plastics, and as a by-product of the manufacture of paints, dyes, and lacquers.

c. 1,3-butadiene is released to the atmosphere naturally during the incomplete combustion of brush and forest fires, and during the burning of biomass, such as wood, leaves, and agricultural materials. It is also produced as a by-product of petroleum refining and the manufacture of plastics and in the exhaust from motor vehicles.

$$H-\overset{\overset{\displaystyle H}{|}}{C}=\overset{\overset{\displaystyle H}{|}}{C}-\overset{\overset{\displaystyle H}{|}}{C}=\overset{\overset{\displaystyle H}{|}}{C}-H$$

d. Methanal is produced naturally as the result of forest fires, in animal wastes, as a product of the microbial breakdown of biological materials, and in the emissions given off by plants. It is also

released from the production and use of a number of synthetic products, such as fiberboard, particleboard, furniture, textiles, glues, and some types of insulation.

7.–11. Student answers will vary.

Changes in the Atmosphere

Exploration Activities

Ozone

1. Earth's primitive atmosphere was a reducing atmosphere, consisting primarily of methane, ammonia, hydrogen, and water, while our modern atmosphere is largely an oxidizing atmosphere, dominated by (inert) nitrogen and oxygen.

2. Ozone is formed when diatomic oxygen is broken apart by solar energy, after which individual oxygen atoms react with diatomic oxygen to form ozone:

   $O_2 \rightarrow 2O$, followed by $O + O_2 + M \rightarrow O_3 + M$.

3. $NO + O_3 \rightarrow NO_2 + O_2$

4. A halogenated hydrocarbon is a hydrocarbon in which one or more hydrogen atoms has been replaced by a halogen atom. A CFC, by contrast, is a halogenated hydrocarbon that contains at least one atom each of chlorine and fluorine.

5. $CCl_2F_2 \xrightarrow{h\upsilon} CClF_2\cdot + Cl\cdot$

   $Cl\cdot + O_3 \rightarrow ClO\cdot + O_2$

   $O_3 \rightarrow O + O_2$ (concurrent with the previous reaction)

$$ClO\cdot + O \rightarrow Cl\cdot + O_2$$

Global Warming

1. CO_2 is removed from the atmosphere largely through the process of photosynthesis: $CO_2 + H_2O \rightarrow (C_6H_{10}O_5)_x + O_2$. It is added to the atmosphere largely through decay and combustion: $(C_6H_{10}O_5)_x + O_2 \rightarrow CO_2 + H_2O$.

2. The atmospheric window is that region of the electromagnetic spectrum between 8,000 and 13,000 nm within which no atmospheric gas absorbs radiation to a significant extent. The atmospheric window provides a mechanism by which heat energy radiated from Earth can escape into space.

3. Student answers may vary, but they will include any activity by which carbon dioxide is released to the atmosphere, such as the combustion of coal, oil, and/or natural gas.

4. The proposed sequence is as follows: Increased production of CO_2 from anthropogenic sources —> Increased concentration of CO_2 in the atmosphere —> Increased amount of heat retained by CO_2 in the atmosphere —> Increase in mean annual temperature of Earth's atmosphere —> Increased melting of polar icecaps and increase in volume of ocean water due to thermal expansion —> Rising level of oceans —> Submersion of coastal areas around the earth —> Dramatic changes in Earth's climatic patterns.

5. Political solutions to the problem of climate change usually involve devising some method of reducing the amount of carbon dioxide released to the atmosphere, such as cutting back on the use of motor vehicles or

on industrial processes in which carbon dioxide is produced. Two technological solutions involve the destruction of CFCs in the atmosphere with laser beams and the stimulation of the growth of phytoplankton in the oceans.

Additional Activities

1.–6. Student answers will vary.

Water Sources

Exploration Activities

The Water Cycle

1. Water evaporates from lakes, rivers, oceans, and other parts of the hydrosphere to become water vapor that becomes part of the atmosphere, either as dispersed water molecules or condensed as tiny droplets of liquid water or ice crystals in clouds. Dispersed water molecules eventually coalesce, condensing on particles of dust or other impurities in the air to form liquid droplets or tiny ice crystals that grow larger by accretion until they are heavy enough to fall back to Earth as precipitation. Precipitation may occur as rain, snow, hail, or sleet, depending on environmental conditions. Some precipitation returns directly to the hydrosphere, completing the water cycle. Other precipitation falls on land, where it may run off the surface into a river or lake or soak into the ground. Water that penetrates the soil becomes groundwater that slowly moves through the earth, returning to the hydrosphere and completing the water cycle.

2. Rainwater is acidic because it dissolves various oxides present in the atmosphere, especially carbon dioxide.

3. Groundwater moves more slowly than water in rivers, and it tends to be more acidic than water in rivers and lakes.

Types of Water Pollutants

1. The categories into which water pollutants can generally be grouped are oxygen-demanding wastes, pathogens, nutrients, synthetic organic compounds, petroleum products, heavy metals, salts, sediments, acidity, radioactive materials, and heat.

2. Answers will vary, but signs of polluted water are fouled stream banks, dead fish, oil-covered beaches, ponds filled with weeds, and smelly rivers.

Oxygen-Demanding Materials

1. Oxygen-demanding wastes can be regarded as water pollutants because they use up oxygen dissolved in water, reducing the amount of life-sustaining oxygen.

2. BOD is the amount of oxygen needed to decompose organic wastes in water.

3. COD measures materials that are not oxidized by bacteria, giving a somewhat different value than BOD.

4. Water is said to be polluted when the measured value of its BOD becomes greater than 5 ppm.

Pathogens

1. Less developed areas tend to have less efficient water purification systems (or none at all) than more developed areas. The most important factor missing in many less developed nations is a system of chlorination that kills waterborne pathogens.

2. The concentration of coliform bacteria provides a rough estimate of the concentration of pathogens in a sample of water.

Additional Activities

Student answers will vary.

Water Pollution

Exploration Activities

Organic Compounds

1. Student answers will vary.

2. SOCs tend to be toxic to plant and animal life and also tend to be very stable.

Synthetic Detergents

1. Soap and surfactant molecules tend to be long, linear molecules with a hydrophobic end and a hydrophilic end.

2. Soaps and syndets remove dirt from materials by forming weak bonds with oily dirt particles at their hydrophobic ends and with water molecules at their hydrophilic ends.

3. Builders soften water and improve the efficiency of cleansing action by removing ions such as Ca^{2+}, Mg^{2+}, Fe^{2+}, and Fe^{3+} from water.

4. Syndets and soaps contain compounds of phosphorus that increase the rate of eutrophication in bodies of water.

Pesticides

1. Some classes of pesticides and the pests against which they are used are the following: avicides: birds; bactericides: bacteria; fungicides: fungi; insecticides: insects; larvicides: larvae; molluscicides: snails and slugs; nematicides: roundworms; rodenticides: rodents; and herbicides: plants.

2. DDT is one of the most effective insecticides ever developed, but it is toxic to some types of organisms; it tends to persist in the environment, and it is especially soluble in

fatty materials, allowing its build-up in animal bodies.

3. Biological magnification is that process by which a contaminant accumulates in the upper levels of a food chain or food web.

4. Some alternative methods of pest control include the use of biological controls, sterilization techniques, plants with greater resistance to insects, and the use of hormones and sex attractants to lure and trap pests.

Petroleum Products

1. The greatest source of petroleum pollution is the release of industrial and motor oils into the environment.

2. The components that make up petroleum have a number of adverse effects on plants and animals. They may kill those organisms outright; they may cause a variety of diseases and other health problems; they may deplete oxygen in bodies of water, causing death by asphyxiation; and they may coat organisms, depriving them of oxygen or causing other health problems.

3. Some of the methods used to prevent or treat oil spills include the use of stronger oil tankers, skimming of oil from the surface of water, adding chemicals that will break down the chemicals in petroleum, adding bacteria that consume petroleum products, and using a variety of devices to frighten organisms away from a polluted area.

Heavy Metals

1. Some elements that are classified as heavy metals are arsenic, beryllium, cadmium, chromium, copper, lead, manganese, molybdenum, and selenium.

2. Lead reacts with sulfhydryl groups in proteins, causing denaturation of the protein and inactivation of their enzymatic action.

3. Elemental mercury and the Hg_2^{2+} ion are only moderately toxic, while the Hg^{2+} ion is very toxic, reacting with sulfhydryl groups and inactivating enzymes.

4. The amount of lead in the environment has been reduced primarily by banning the use of leaded compounds in internal combustion fuels. It has also been reduced by banning the use of lead compounds in the manufacture of most kinds of paint.

Other Metal Pollutants

1. Mobilization is the process by which a metal tied up in some insoluble form is converted to a soluble form. The presence of acids in soil can cause this transformation.

2. Aluminum can enter the roots of plants and disrupt normal growth and development. Aluminum has also been implicated in the human disorder Alzheimer's disease, although the connection is uncertain at this point.

3. Mobilization can occur if acidified water is passed through a water distribution system containing copper piping. Copper may dissolve in water with an acidic pH, forming Cu_2+ ions, which may cause damage to plants and algae.

Sedimentation

1. As a rule of thumb, soil is washed off cultivated land five to 10 times as fast as it is off noncultivated land, 100 times as fast off land on which construction is taking place, and more than 500 times as fast on mined land.

2. Two mechanisms that result in the formation of sediments in water are represented by the following equations:

   (1) $CO_2(aq) + H_2O \rightleftarrows H^+(aq) + HCO_3^-(aq)$, followed by

   $Ca^{2+}(aq) + 2HCO_3^-(aq) \rightleftarrows CaCO_3(s) + CO_2(aq) + H_2O$, and

   (2) $4Fe^{2+}(aq) + 4H^+(aq) + O_2(g) \rightarrow 4Fe^{3+} + 2H_2O$, followed by $Fe^{3+}(aq) + 3H_2O \rightarrow Fe(OH)_3(s) + 3H^+(aq)$

3. Sediments can reduce the amount of light and oxygen available to aquatic organisms, and they may, in some cases, carry toxic materials adhered to their surfaces.

Salinity

1. The salinity of freshwater lakes ranges from about 150 mg TDS/L to about 4,000 mg TDS/L. In comparison, the salinity of ocean water ranges from 18,000 to 35,000 mg TDS/L.

2. In most lakes and ponds, salinity remains about constant because fresh water from rivers and streams replaces water lost by evaporation.

3. Human activities that increase salinity include the salting of roads during winter months, agricultural operations, and a high domestic demand for fresh water.

Heat

1. Heated water is able to dissolve less oxygen than cooler water, posing a threat to aquatic organisms that require oxygen for their survival. In addition, many organisms are adapted for life within a relatively narrow temperature range. Heated water can affect the migration and spawning patterns of fish.

2. Two alternatives are the construction of huge cooling towers through which effluent water can be pumped and the diversion of warm wastewater to ponds filled with organisms that thrive at higher temperatures. Student opinions will vary.

Additional Activities

Student answers will vary.

Solid Wastes

Exploration Activities

Introduction

1. The two largest sources of solid wastes in the United States are agricultural activities and mining.

2. These sources are generally not considered as serious an environmental problem as other sources because they tend to be located on relatively remote areas of land where they have relatively little direct impact on human populations.

Wastes From Mining Operations

1. Some companies prefer to pay the fines charged for violating the law rather than pay the cost of restoring the damaged land.

2. The EPA defines a hazardous waste as any substance that is flammable, corrosive, reactive, or toxic.

3. $4FeS_2 + 15O_2 + 14H_2O \rightarrow 4Fe(OH)_3 + 8H_2SO_4$

Agricultural Wastes

1. Manure and plant wastes provide an ideal breeding ground for pathogenic organisms. These organisms may be transmitted to humans or other animals.

2. Often, the places where such fertilizers would be in the greatest demand are often

far removed from the feedlots where they are produced.

Municipal and Industrial Sources

1. PCBs tend to be very stable, fat-soluble, and toxic. The first property (along with other PCB properties), makes them valuable in many industrial applications, but the combination of these three properties makes them a potential threat to the health of humans and other animals.

2. The top 10 toxic pollutants, as defined by the EPA, are arsenic, lead, mercury, vinyl chloride, polychlorinated biphenyls (PCBs), benzene, cadmium, benzo(αH)pyrene, polycyclic aromatic hydrocarbons (PAHs), and benzo(βH)fluoranthene.

Disposal

1. A sanitary landfill is a disposal site where layers of clean earth are added periodically on top of layers of compacted municipal wastes and, in some cases, additional precautions are taken to prevent the escape of wastes from the landfill into the surrounding environment. An open dump has no provisions for containing such wastes within the dumping area.

2. Incineration is a relatively simple and effective method for disposing of solid wastes in which the energy produced can be used as a source of heat for a variety of purposes. The disadvantage of incineration is that toxic and hazardous gases may be released to the surrounding environment.

3. One method of recycling is simply to reuse a product more than once, as is done when grocery bags are reused. Another form of recycling involves melting down waste products (such as glass or metal) and reusing them in the manufacture of new products. A third form of recycling involves chemical and/or physical changes in a material that allow it to be used in a new and different type of product, as in the use of waste paper to make petroleum.

4. One method of reducing the hazards of wastes is through neutralization, as represented by either of the following equations:

$$2H^+(aq) + Ca(OH)_2(s) \rightarrow Ca^{2+}(aq) + 2H_2O$$
$$2OH^-(aq) + H_2SO_4(aq) + 2H_2O + SO_4^{2-}(aq),$$

or through an oxidation reaction, such as:

$$2CN^-(aq) + Cl_2(g) + 2OH^-(aq) \rightarrow 2CNO^-(aq) + H_2(g) + 2Cl^-(aq)$$

or by a precipitation reaction, such as:

$$8CrO_4^{2-}(aq) + 15S^{2-}(aq) + 20H_2O \rightarrow 4Cr_2S_3(s) + 3SO_4^{2-}(aq) + 40OH^-(aq)$$

5. Deep-well injection can be used in an area where a permeable zone of rock is sandwiched between two impermeable layers above and below it.

Additional Activities

Student answers will vary.

Resources

Books

Bailey, Ronald Albert, et al. *Chemistry of the Environment,* 2nd edition. New York: Academic Press, 2002.

Baird, Colin. *Environmental Chemistry,* 2nd edition. New York: W. H. Freeman & Co., 1998.

Benjamin, Mark M. *Water Chemistry.* New York: McGraw Hill Science/Engineering/Math, 2001.

Harrison, Roy M. *Pollution: Causes, Effects, and Control,* 4th edition. Cambridge, UK: Royal Society of Chemistry, 2001.

Jacobson, Mark Z. *Atmospheric Pollution.* Cambridge: Cambridge University Press, 2002.

Manahan, Stanley E. *Environmental Chemistry,* 4th edition. Boca Raton, FL: Lewis Publishers, 1999.

Manahan, Stanley E. *Fundamentals of Environmental Chemistry,* 2nd edition. Boca Raton, FL: Lewis Publishers, 2000.

Schwedt, Georg. *The Essential Guide to Environmental Chemistry.* New York: John Wiley & Sons, 2002.

Spiro, Thomas G., and William M. Stigliani. *Chemistry of the Environment,* 2nd edition. Upper Saddle River, NJ: Prentice-Hall, 2003.

Spiro, Thomas G., and Zafra Leman. *From Ozone to Oil Spills: Chemistry, the Environment, and You.* New York: Macmillan Technical Publishing, 2004.

Wright, John. *Environmental Chemistry.* London: Routledge, 2002.

Vanloon, Gary W., and Stephen J. Duffy. *Environmental Chemistry: A Global Perspective.* Oxford: Oxford University Press, 2000.

Web Sites

Countless web sites are available that contain information on various aspects of environmental chemistry. The following are a few from which you can begin more detailed searches of the Internet.

Environmental Defense Fund
www.environmentaldefense.org/home.cfm

Friends of the Earth
www.foe.org

Greenpeace
www.greenpeaceusa.org

National Environmental Data Index
www.nedi.gov/databases.html

National Oceanic and Atmospheric Administration
www.noaa.gov

Natural Resources Defense Council
www.nrdc.org/nrdc

United Nations Environment Programme
www.unep.org

U.S. Environmental Protection Agency
www.epa.gov

Time Line of Environmental Chemistry

1306—King Edward I prohibits the use of coals for fires declaring that "whosoever shall be found guilty of burning coal shall suffer the loss of his head."

1661—Englishman John Evelyn writes a tract about the foul air of London, entitled *Fumifugium,* which he directs to the attention of King Charles II. Evelyn explains that the purpose of his tract is to show "how this pernicious Nuisance [air pollution] may be reformed; and [to show how]. . . the Aer may not only be freed from the present Inconveniency; but (that remov'd) to render not only Your Majesties Palace, but the whole City likewise, one of the sweetest, and most delicious Habitations in the World."

1848—England adopts the world's first Public Health Act, establishing a Health Agency whose responsibility it is to control the release of smoke and ash in English cities. The first person specifically responsible for air pollution control, Robert Angus Smith, is not appointed for another 24 years.

1853—In one of the earliest and most famous examples of the way in which epidemiology can be used to trace the course of disease, an English physician by the name of John Snow determines that the cause of a cholera epidemic in London is a public well that has become contaminated by sewage. Snow advises that the only way to stop the epidemic is to remove the pump handle from the well. Authorities do so, and the epidemic dies out.

1880—London is covered with an unusually heavy blanket of smog, resulting in the death of more than 1,000 individuals.

1899—The U.S. Congress passes the Rivers and Harbors Act (also known as the Refuse Act of 1899). The act is designed to deal with problems of navigation, disease, and oil discharges in navigable waters. Some sections of the act, dealing with the construction of dams, bridges, dikes, causeways, wharfs, piers, and other structures, are still being used today to deal with certain kinds of modern water issues.

1926—The first environmental act in the Western world of any actual practical consequence, England's Public Health (Smoke Abatement) Act, is adopted.

1930—Air pollution in the Meuse valley, Belgium, results in the death of 63 individuals.

1948—The U.S. Congress passes the Water Pollution Control Act, also known as the Clean Water Act. The Water Pollution Control Act and its immediate successors, adopted in 1961, 1966, and 1970, are largely unsuccessful in dealing with the nation's water pollution problems.

1952—An unusually severe period of smoggy weather in London results in perhaps the worst such event in modern history, with more than 4,000 deaths attributed to polluted air.

1955—The first air pollution control act, the Air Pollution Control Act of 1955, is adopted in the United States. Like the Water Pollution Control Act of 1948, it is very weak and does virtually nothing to deal with the nation's air pollution problems. Amendments adopted to the act in 1965, 1966, 1967, and 1969 provide minimal improvements over the original act.

1962—A book by Rachel Carson, *Silent Spring,* calls attention to the dangers of careless use of pesticides and dramatically increases the awareness of the American public about this and related environmental problems.

1970—(January 1) National Environmental Policy Act of 1970 is passed in the United States. The act creates the nation's first federal environmental agency, the Environmental Protection Agency (EPA).

1970—(April 22) The nation's first Earth Day is held throughout the United States, with a variety of efforts to increase the American public's awareness of environmental problems.

1970—The U.S. Congress adopts the Clean Air Act of 1970, which turns out to be one of the first really effective pieces of legislation in terms of environmental protection. Major amendments strengthening the act are adopted in 1955, 1963, 1970, and 1990.

1972—In an effort to deal with pollution of the nation's waterways, The U.S. Congress adopts the Federal Water Pollution Control Act (later renamed the Clean Water Act). The act was later revised and amended a number of times, most importantly in 1977, 1981, 1987, 1990, and 2002.

1972—The U.S. Congress passes the Federal Insecticide, Fungicide, and Rodenticide Act, requirng the EPA to study the consequences of pesticide usage and to require users (such as farmers) to register when purchasing pesticides.

1972—The use of DDT is banned in the United States.

1972—The first bottle recycling bill is passed in Oregon.

1973—The Endangered Species Act is passed, authorizing the U.S. Fish and Wildlife Service to create and maintain a list of endangered plant and animal species and to take such actions as are necessary to protect those species, within certain limitations.

1974—The Safe Drinking Water Act is adopted, requiring the EPA to set national standards for drinking water that will protect the general public against both naturally occurring and human-made contaminants that might be found in drinking water.

1974—F. Sherwood Rowland and Mario J. Molina hypothesize a mechanism by which chlorofluorocarbons destroy ozone in the stratosphere.

1976—The U.S. Congress passes the Toxic Substances Control Act, giving the EPA authority to screen and monitor the use of more than 75,000 industrial chemicals produced, used in, and imported into the United States.

1976—A federal court authorizes the EPA to begin the elimination of leaded fuel in the United States.

1976—An explosion at a Hoffman-LaRoche chemical plant in Seveso, Italy, injures about 30 people and causes chloracne, a severe skin disease, in over 300 school children.

1977—The Resource Conservation and Recovery Act is adopted in the United States, establishing programs for the monitoring and control of hazardous and nonhazardous wastes and their disposal.

1977—The U.S. Congress passes the Soil and Water Conservation Act and the Surface Mining Control and Reclamation Act.

1978—President Jimmy Carter declares a state of emergency at Love Canal, in Niagara Falls, New York, when studies show land in the area has been severely polluted by the dumping of hazardous wastes by the Hooker Chemical Company.

1979—The worst nuclear disaster in U.S. history occurs when the reactor core at the Three Mile Island (Pennsylvania) nuclear power plant almost suffers a complete meltdown.

1979—Robert Bullard and his wife file a law suit against the city of Houston, Texas, charging that Browning Ferris Industries, one of the largest national waste companies, is practicing "environmental racism" in the siting of their landfills for hazardous wastes by locating such landfills in areas that are occupied primarily by people of color and poor people. The action becomes one of the signal moments in the rise of the *environmental justice* movement.

1980—The U.S. Congress adopts the Comprehensive Environmental Response, Compensation, and Liability Act, creating a program known as Superfund, designed to clean up hazardous waste sites as well as accidents, spills, and other emergency releases of pollutants into the environment.

1980—The U.S. Congress passes National Security Act of 1980, which includes a requirement that all gasoline be blended with a minimum of 10 percent grain alcohol, otherwise known as *gasohol*. The requirement is later overturned by the administration of President Ronald Reagan.

1981—The Task Force on Regulatory Relief, chaired by Vice President George Bush, recommends that the phaseout of leaded gasoline be eliminated or slowed down.

1984—A fertilizer plant operated by Union Carbide Company in Bhopal, India, leaks the toxic chemical methyl icocyanide, resulting in about 2,000 deaths of poisoning, an additional 8,000 deaths from chronic effects, and an estimated 100,000 health injuries.

1985—British scientist Joseph Farman reports the discovery of a hole in the ozone layer over Antarctica.

1986—The Number Four reactor at the Chernobyl Nuclear Power Plant near Kiev explodes and catches fire. Within a few days, at least 31 people died and untold thousands were exposed to high doses of radiation.

1987—The Montreal Protocol on Substances that Deplete the Ozone Layer is signed by 24 countries, including the United States. The Protocol is later amended by actions taken in London in 1990 and Copenhagen in 1992.

1988—The World Meteorological Organization and the United Nations Environmental Programme establish a program—the Intergovernmental Panel on Climate Change (IPCC)—for studying trends in global warming and possible social, economic, and environmental consequences of such changes.

1989—The United Nations adopts the Basel Convention on the Control of Transboundary Movements of Hazardous Wastes and Their Disposal, an act designed to reduce the dumping of hazardous wastes in less developed nations.

1992—The United Nations Conference on Environment and Development (UNCED), informally known as the Earth Summit, is held in Rio de Janeiro.

1994—Robert Bullard publishes *Dumping in Dixie: Class and Environmental Quality,* one of the most important works of the young environmental justice movement.

1997—The Kyoto Protocol is signed by 122 nations, including the United States, in an effort to reduce the amount of greenhouse gases released to the atmosphere. The United States Congress later indicates that it has no intention of ratifying the agreement.

2000—The European Union bans leaded gasoline in its member nations.

2001—The National Research Council publishes a report, *Abrupt Climate Change: Inevitable Surprises,* suggesting that climate change is likely to arrive very quickly, resulting in sudden and catastrophic damage to people, property, and natural ecosystems.

2001—The World Meteorological Organization publishes a report predicting that 2001 will be the second warmest on record. Nine of the 10 warmest years reported since international records were first kept in 1860 occurred between 1990 and 2001. This prediction was later confirmed to be correct.

2002—The World Summit on Sustainable Development is held in Johannesburg, South Africa, with disappointing results. Venezuela's President Hugo Chavez calls the meeting "a dialogue of the deaf."

2003—In an effort to lessen the economic impact of some previous environmental legislation, the administration of U.S. President George W. Bush recommends a weakening of certain environmental legislation, including the Clean Air Act, the Clean Water Act, the Superfund program, and protection of wild and natural areas.

acid rain: rain that has a pH significantly lower than that of natural rain

aliphatic hydrocarbon: compound containing only carbon and hydrogen and having a molecular structure consisting exclusively of open chains

alkane: hydrocarbon containing only carbon–carbon single bonds; also known as a **saturated hydrocarbon**

alkene: hydrocarbon containing at least one carbon–carbon double bond; also called an **unsaturated hydrocarbon**

anthropogenic: produced as the result of human actions

aromatic hydrocarbon: compound containing only carbon and hydrogen and having a molecular structure similar to that of benzene (a ring)

atmosphere: envelope of gases that surrounds Earth's surface

atmospheric window: portion of the atmosphere's absorption spectrum between 8,000 and 13,000 nm through which radiation can normally escape

biochemical oxygen demand: measure of organic contamination in water as measured by the amount of oxygen consumed by microorganisms over a standard period of time at a standard temperature

biodegradable: able to break down naturally in the environment as the result of microbial action

biological magnification: process by which a contaminant accumulates in the upper levels of a food chain or food web

biosphere: the part of the earth that consists of all living organisms

builder: chemical in synthetic detergents that binds to Ca^{2+}, Mg^{2+}, and other ions that cause hardness in water, thus improving the action of a surfactant

catalytic converter: a device in a motor vehicle's exhaust system that converts pollutants such as carbon monoxide, hydrocarbons, and nitrogen oxides to harmless gases

chemical oxygen demand: measure of organic contamination present in water, as determined by treatment with a strong oxidizing agent

coliform bacteria: bacteria that live naturally in the human digestive system and can be used to measure the concentration of pathogens in a sample of water

contaminant: any material that is not normally present in the environment, but, when present, is harmless to humans and other organisms

detergent: cleaning agent

dry deposition: process by which particles are removed from the atmosphere without the intervention of snow, rain, or other forms of wet precipitation

dump: any place where solid wastes are disposed of

environmental chemistry: study of chemical species that occur in the environment and the interactions that take place among them

eutrophication: process by which the concentration of nutrients in a lake increases, promoting the growth of plant life and the evolution of the lake to a wetlands and, eventually, to a meadow

fecal coliform count: number of coliform bacteria, found in a sample, that originated specifically from feces

feedlot: area where animals are penned up and food is brought to them, in contrast with the traditional practice of having animals forage for their own food

fly ash: very finely divided solid produced during the combustion of coal

fossil fuel: term used to describe coal, oil, and/or natural gas

gasification: process by which solid coal is converted to a synthetic gaseous fuel

half-life: the time it takes for the concentration of some substance to be reduced by half in a biological system

halogenated hydrocarbons: hydrocarbons that contain one or more halogen atoms substituted for one or more hydrogen atoms in their molecules

hazardous waste: any waste product that is flammable, corrosive, reactive, or toxic

heavy metal: any metal that, in greater than trace amounts, is toxic to plants, humans, or other organisms

hydrosphere: the oceans, lakes, rivers, polar ice caps, groundwater, glaciers, and other water that exists on the earth

industrial smog: form of air pollution resulting from the combination of smoke and fog

limiting factor: any condition that controls the growth or abundance of an organism or group of organisms

lithosphere: the solid portion of the earth

mesosphere: layer of the atmosphere above the stratosphere and below the thermosphere

micronutrient: element needed in very small amounts to maintain the health of an organism

mobilization: process by which a metal that is tied up in some insoluble form is converted to a soluble form

nonrenewable resource: any resource that, once used up, cannot be replaced readily by natural processes

particulates: particles that occur in the atmosphere as the result of either natural or anthropogenic causes

pathogens: disease-causing organisms

photochemical oxidants: compounds produced as the result of the reaction among hydrocarbons, nitrogen oxides, and ozone in photochemical smog

photochemical smog: form of air pollution that occurs when hydrocarbons and oxides of nitrogen are converted to noxious chemicals by sunlight

photolytic reaction: decomposition reaction catalyzed by radiation

photosynthesis: process by which green plants use sunlight to convert carbon dioxide and water to carbohydrates and oxygen

pollutant: any contaminant that occurs in high enough concentration to present a health risk to plants, humans, or other organisms

primary pollutants: pollutants emitted directly from some anthropogenic source

primary standards: air quality standards designed to protect the health of humans

sanitary landfill: dump that consists of alternate layers of compacted solid wastes and clean soil

saturated hydrocarbon: see alkane

secondary pollutants: pollutants produced as the result of the reaction among anthropogenic contaminants and naturally occurring compounds

secondary standards: air quality standards designed to protect parts of the environment other than human health

secure landfill: a sanitary landfill that contains a bottom lining designed to prevent leakage of materials into the ground

sediments: solid materials that settle out of water or air

sink: final location in which a contaminant or pollutant is deposited for an extended period of time

stratopause: region of the atmosphere that separates the stratosphere and mesosphere

stratosphere: region of the atmosphere above the troposphere and below the mesosphere

surfactant: component of a synthetic detergent that acts as an emulsifying agent between oil-covered dirt and water

synthetic detergents: cleaning agents consisting of a surfactant, a builder, and other synthetic organic compounds

synthetic organic compounds: compounds invented by chemists

tailings: wastes produced during the processing of ores

technosphere: the part of the environment produced by human activities, such as plastics, synthetic fabrics, alloys, wood products, paper, and glass

terpenes: naturally occurring hydrocarbons that usually contain 10, 15, 20, or 30 carbon atoms

thermal pollution: warming of water as the result of human activities

thermosphere: highest region of the atmosphere

total coliform count: total number of coliform from all sources found in a sample, as distinguished from fecal coliform count

total organic carbon: method of measuring organic contamination of water based on the high-temperature combustion of solids taken from a water sample

tropopause: region between the troposphere and stratosphere in the atmosphere

troposphere: lowest shell of the atmosphere, where the vast majority of human activity takes place

tropospheric lapse rate: regular decrease in temperature of about 9.8°C/km that occurs within the troposphere

unsaturated hydrocarbon: see alkene

volatile organic compound: carbon-containing compound that exists as a gas or vaporizes easily

water cycle: sequence of chemical and physical changes that occur as water moves through the hydrosphere, atmosphere, and lithosphere

wet deposition: removal of particles from the atmosphere by means of snow, rain, and other forms of wet precipitation

WALCH PUBLISHING

Share Your Bright Ideas

We want to hear from you!

Your name_____Date_____

School name_____

School address_____

City _____State _____Zip_____Phone number (_____)_____

Grade level(s) taught_____Subject area(s) taught_____

Where did you purchase this publication?_____

In what month do you purchase a majority of your supplements?_____

What moneys were used to purchase this product?

____School supplemental budget   ____Federal/state funding   ____Personal

Please "grade" this Walch publication in the following areas:

Quality of service you received when purchasing	A	B	C	D
Ease of use	A	B	C	D
Quality of content	A	B	C	D
Page layout	A	B	C	D
Organization of material	A	B	C	D
Suitability for grade level	A	B	C	D
Instructional value	A	B	C	D

COMMENTS:_____

_____

What specific supplemental materials would help you meet your current—or future—instructional needs?

_____

Have you used other Walch publications? If so, which ones?_____

May we use your comments in upcoming communications?   ____Yes   ____No

Please **FAX** this completed form to **888-991-5755**, or mail it to

Customer Service, Walch Publishing, P. O. Box 658, Portland, ME 04104-0658

We will send you a **FREE GIFT** in appreciation of your feedback. **THANK YOU!**